Developing Teams

George Green

- Fast-track route to building a cohesive and effective team

- Covers analysis of the contributions of team members and team leaders, and how they interact

- Case studies of the Republic of Ireland soccer team demonstrating how team spirit can help to drive a team to perform beyond expectations, the partnership between the North American Space Agency and Russian Space Agency exploring the international aspects of team working, and Raffles hotel, Singapore, showing the importance of culture to a team

- Includes a comprehensive resources guide, key concepts and thinkers, a 10-step action plan for team development, and a section of FAQs

TRAINING & DEVELOPMENT

11.06

Copyright © Capstone Publishing, 2003

The right of George Green to be identified as the author of this book has been asserted in accordance with the Copyright, Designs and Patents Act 1988

First Published 2003 by
Capstone Publishing Limited (a Wiley company)
8 Newtec Place
Magdalen Road
Oxford OX4 1RE
United Kingdom
http://www.capstoneideas.com

CIP catalogue records for this book are available from the British Library and the US Library of Congress

ISBN 1-84112-447-8

Printed and bound in Great Britain by CPI Antony Rowe, Eastbourne

Wiley also publishes its books in a variety of electronic formats. Some content that appears in print may not be available in electronic books.

Websites often change their contents and addresses; details of sites listed in this book were accurate at the time of writing, but may change.

Substantial discounts on bulk quantities of Capstone Books are available to corporations, professional associations and other organizations. For details telephone Capstone Publishing on (+44-1865-798623), fax (+44-1865-240941) or email (info@wiley-capstone.co.uk).

Contents

Introduction to ExpressExec

ExpressExec is a completely up-to-date resource of current business practice, accessible in a number of ways – anytime, anyplace, anywhere. ExpressExec combines best practice cases, key ideas, action points, glossaries, further reading, and resources.

Each module contains 10 individual titles that cover all the key aspects of global business practice. Written by leading experts in their field, the knowledge imparted provides executives with the tools and skills to increase their personal and business effectiveness, benefiting both employee and employer.

ExpressExec is available in a number of formats:

» **Print** – 120 titles available through retailers or printed on demand using any combination of the 1200 chapters available.
» **E-Books** – e-books can be individually downloaded from ExpressExec.com or online retailers onto PCs, handheld computers, and e-readers.
» **Online** – http://www.expressexec.wiley.com/ provides fully searchable access to the complete ExpressExec resource via the Internet – a cost-effective online tool to increase business expertise across a whole organization.

» **ExpressExec Performance Support Solution (EEPSS)** – a software solution that integrates ExpressExec content with interactive tools to provide organizations with a complete internal management development solution.

» **ExpressExec Rights and Syndication** – ExpressExec content can be licensed for translation or display within intranets or on Internet sites.

To find out more visit www.ExpressExec.com or contact elound@wiley-capstone.co.uk.

Introduction

This chapter looks at the role of teams in the modern world. It considers:

» the growing recognition by organizations of the value of teamwork;
» the reasons why developing teams is important;
» the application of the concepts to any field of activity; and
» the value of team spirit.

Until the late 1970s, the context in which people most frequently referred to "teams" was in the field of sport, rather than business. Each player or competitor would be chosen for their strength in a particular position, activity, or skill. Since then, however, teamwork has become an increasingly important concept within many of the most successful organizations in the global marketplace. The phrase "team building" is now part of the normal vocabulary of organizational life. More recently the media has noted the potential interest in the ways in which groups of people interact, as shown by television series such as *Big Brother* and *The Weakest Link*.

Most effective organizations today include in their mission statements a specific reference to the value of "effective teams." Because of the competitive nature of the world today, each organization – whether it be profit-seeking, not- for- profit, charitable, or political – needs to deliver the best service it possibly can to its customers. To do that, it needs to manage and develop the skills of its people in the most effective way.

Most business processes require the involvement of more than one person, whether as a result of complexity or output volume. Successful organizations recognize that they are more likely to succeed if they encourage their people to work together in cohesive teams, which help and support each other in delivering the end product to the customer. Thereby, the development of effective teams has become just as important as the development of effective individuals.

The term "synergy" is often used to describe the effect that a team can produce, and is often expressed as $2 + 2 = 5$, suggesting that a team will deliver more as a unit than each of its members could deliver separately. Another phrase which is often used to describe this phenomenon is "team spirit."

One good example is the way this "team spirit" or "synergy" was demonstrated by two teams at the 2002 World Cup: the Republic of Ireland and South Korea. Before the tournament, the Irish team was widely regarded as a good one, though not perhaps as skilful as some of its potential opponents. Few teams relished the idea of playing against Ireland, however, because of its famous "team spirit," which invariably sees the team play to a higher level than seems possible considering the individual skill level of each player. This "invisible force" also meant that the team never gave up, even when games appeared lost, believing to the very last kick that they could triumph. This was particularly noticeable when they equalized the scoring with Germany in the group stages with a goal in the last minute of added time – no mean feat as Germany went on to be runners up in the competition. (We will look at this team in more detail in a case study in Chapter 7.) The co-hosts South Korea also showed great team spirit by reaching the semi-finals when they had never previously won a game at the World Cup final stages.

Such team spirit is not confined to the soccer pitch or the sporting arena (indeed, most sports are now considered to be businesses and many soccer clubs in the UK, for example, are public companies); it can be very evident in all types of organization and then it makes a real difference for customers. However, it will not develop by accident; the organization needs to establish a climate in which it can grow. Over the next few chapters we will be looking at what can be done to develop teams so that they can deliver a performance that is over and above expectation.

We will also see, in Chapter 7, some specific examples of teams that perform to the very highest standards.

What Do We Mean By "Developing Teams"?

This chapter explores the meaning of the expression "developing teams" in this context. It considers:

» what constitutes a team;
» objectives of teams;
» types of team;
» organizing teams;
» what teams do;
» leadership;
» team dynamics;
» the size of a team;
» team evolution; and
» training and development.

Before we can begin to develop a team, we need to be clear about what a team is. Let's begin with a definition.

WHAT IS A TEAM?

Early usage of the word "team" related to horses "pulling together" to draw a plough or a stagecoach; or to dogs "pulling together" on a sled. Both the horses and the dogs were all pulling in the same direction to reach a common destination – if they didn't, they would probably pull in different directions and end up getting nowhere.

The ideas of "pulling together" and "common destination" provide a good starting point from which to explore what teams of people are and what can be done to develop them into an effective force for an organization. So we might begin by describing a team as "a group of people pulling together for a common purpose."

In sport, the common purpose of a team is often quite clear – to win the race, the competition, the game, the league, the cup, or whatever, depending on the sporting activity. However, in business, the common purpose of a team is rarely as clear and it may be worthwhile ensuring that everyone in the team knows what it is.

There may be another factor to consider too. Most sportsmen and women might be very clear about the value to themselves as individuals of achieving the common purpose of winning the game or competition; you only have to look at the joyful faces of winning competitors. In business, however, although people may know the common purpose of their organization, this does not automatically mean that they will value the achievement of that purpose. Therefore, it may be necessary to motivate people to achieve the desired result. We will look at motivation in more detail in Chapter 6.

So, perhaps we might add to our earlier definition of the team and describe it as "a group of people pulling together for a common purpose, *which they value.*"

OBJECTIVES

Almost every successful organization will have a mission statement that outlines exactly what its purpose is. Although this is usually a broad statement of intent, it is extremely important because it sets out a map that shows people where it should be operating and where it should not.

Thus an organization might want to be the best in the world, or the best in Japan. Although the word "best" is quite vague and needs to be defined more specifically through the identification of SMART objectives (see below), the sphere of operations is quite clear and any teams which step outside the boundary are likely to be working outside the organization's key purpose.

It can be a good idea for each team to have its own mission statement, so its members are always reminded about its purpose. This purpose should be translated into specific objectives so that the team knows exactly what it has to achieve. The objectives, themselves, should be SMART, that is:

» **S**pecific – so what has to be achieved is clear;
» **M**easurable – so the team knows when it has achieved it;
» **A**greed – so the team takes ownership of the objective;
» **R**ealistic – so the team feels motivated and has a "can do" attitude; and
» **T**ime-bound – so the deadline is clear.

The team's performance against these objectives should be regularly monitored and feedback should be given to the team members about what is being done well and what needs to be improved.

As well as being realistic, the objectives should be challenging, in order to stretch the team.

TYPES OF TEAM

There are many types of team, including the following.

» Teams that are organized to work closely with one another on a full-time basis as part of a function or department of a business. They communicate through agreed procedures, regular channels, and day-to-day contact.
» Teams that are set up to carry out a specific project and will disband at the end of it. As above, they communicate through agreed procedures and day-to-day contact, though they may often use unorthodox channels to clear blockages in the project.

» Teams that meet regularly at periods of several months, but rarely meet in between, such as working committees. Communication occurs through the meetings, formal minutes issued afterwards, and subsequent contact between specific individuals who need to take joint action as a result (these teams are known as secondary teams).
» Informal groups that flourish within an organization and are not bound by any considerations of hierarchy or departmental alignment. Here, communication will be by word of mouth, grapevine, and gossip!

ORGANIZING TEAMS

In any organization, there may be a need for several teams (in larger ones, perhaps even hundreds or thousands of them). The way in which people are divided into their teams may be decided by a number of factors, including:

» the types of activity carried out by the organization;
» the variety of customers it has;
» the size of the organization;
» the number of locations in which it operates;
» specific skills needed to supply a particular product or service;
» deadlines for production; and
» administrative functions needed to support the core product.

Typically, a large organization might be hierarchical in nature, organized into departments according to function – such as human resource, finance, or operations departments; geographical location – such as UK, US, Japan; or product – such as product 1, 2, or 3.

These may be further split into smaller teams based around particular locations or activities:

» **Human resource**: training, recruitment, and salaries/wages;
» **Finance**: accounts receivable, accounts payable, and budgets;
» **Operations**: production, supply, planning, and maintenance;
» **Japan Office**: Tokyo, Yokohama, and Kyoto offices;
» **Product 1**: marketing, sales, and dispatch.

Depending upon the size of the organization, these teams may be subdivided even further to ensure that they are of an effective size for the task in hand. Each of these are usually managed or supervised by a team leader.

Thus, in a very large organization, the human resource manager may manage a team that includes the training, recruitment and salaries/wages managers, each of whom manage several teams, each of which also have a team leader. Usually, each team member will have a specific role or roles, which set out what his or her contribution to the task is going to be. It is usually based upon that person's knowledge and areas of skill. We can call this the **functional team role**.

Some organizations employ what is termed a "matrix" structure, in which they set up teams comprising people from a variety of functional, geographical, or product-determined areas so that they have enough expertise to make decisions for themselves, without having to refer to other departments for advice. Thus, a company which is designing cars might set up a team with members from design, production, sales, human resources, and engineering. The team will have sufficient skills and knowledge to make a significant number of crucial decisions without waiting for advice through the usual departmental channels. Each team member will also have a direct line to his or her own function so that any advice that is still needed can be accessed very quickly. We will see a good example of this in Chapter 7, when we look at the collaboration between the North American Space Agency (NASA) and the Russian Space Agency (RSA).

In these structures, authority for decision making is often passed down to the team itself, which, as we will see further in Chapter 6, can be a very motivating factor in itself.

WHAT TEAMS DO

There are many activities that take place within teams. Here we consider and define some of them.

» **Exchanging information internally** – sharing information with each other within the team.
» **Exchanging information externally** – exchanging relevant information with people from outside the team.

» **Distributing work** – identifying who has the time and the knowledge or skills to carry out a particular task.
» **Building internal relationships** – individual team members need to get to know one another so that they are aware of the knowledge and skills possessed by other team members.
» **Building external relationships** – it is very likely that the team will need the help of other people to meet its own objectives. These may be other people in the department or organization, or they may be people in other organizations.
» **Making decisions** – the team may have all of the knowledge and skills needed, or it may have to seek advice from other people.
» **Generating new ideas** – an effective team will create an environment in which no ideas are rejected out of hand, no matter how outlandish they may at first appear. This allows the team to think differently and be ahead of its competitors.
» **Troubleshooting** – putting things right when they go wrong. This could relate to errors or delays in the task itself or to conflict between individuals either within or outside the team.
» **Reviewing performance** – all teams need to review their performance at frequent intervals to ensure that they are still on track.

We need to recognize that the delivery of specific services to customers or end users may be delegated to sub-teams or to individual members of the team. The rest of the team need to ensure that a mechanism for contact and support is maintained throughout this time.

LEADERSHIP

Many organizations recognize the importance of good leadership at every level. Leadership is generally considered to be about using your skills to *influence* people to act in a particular way; unlike power, which is about using a variety of means to *force* someone to do what you want.

Of course, leadership may also mean different things to people in different parts of the organization. For example, at the very top, the most important factor may be that the leader has a vision of the future of the organization. John Adair, a leading writer on teams and leadership, argues in his book *Great Leaders* (1990) that a strategic leader needs to:

» have a clear sense of direction which team members can embrace;
» be a good team builder, especially in terms of objectives and communication; and
» be creative and encourage creativity among others.

At the lower levels of the organization, however, the key factors may be that the leader is available to talk to when there is a problem or is prepared to take account of other people's views when making decisions.

When team members are asked what they expect from a leader, the most common responses include:

» a sense of purpose;
» listening skills;
» integrity;
» resolution;
» clarity of thinking;
» fairness;
» availability;
» flexibility to change their minds;
» preparedness to get to know the team;
» vision.

There are many very interesting theories of leadership, some of which we will look at in more detail in Chapter 3 and Chapter 8.

TEAM DYNAMICS

If there is a team leader, it follows that there will be team members, so let's now look more closely about how team members might behave.

We will see, in Chapter 3, that there has been a lot of investigation into team dynamics. Many teams become ineffective because they can't find a way of working together without conflict that deflects them from their task. Other teams simply give up because they can't find the determination to meet their deadline.

Meredith Belbin (1981) suggests that, in addition to functional roles, which we referred to earlier in this chapter, a successful team also needs to demonstrate additional attributes in order for it to perform well as a cohesive team. He refers to these as **natural team roles**.

Belbin identifies nine such roles, all of which must be represented in the team if it is to perform well. Each team member may be able to take on more than one role, so even small teams can conform to this ideal. (We will look at the nine natural team roles in more detail in Chapter 3 and Chapter 8.)

THE SIZE OF A TEAM

Belbin suggests that to ensure effective working relationships the optimum team size may be between three and five, with each member performing more than one of the nine natural team roles. However, team size may also depend on the number of functional roles that are needed, which will be affected by the complexity of the activities that it has to carry out and by the variety of skills and knowledge that it needs in order to carry them out. In team sports such as soccer, for example, there are eleven functional roles to be filled at any given time during the game.

The size of the team, therefore, will depend upon three main factors:

» the number and complexity of the activities to be carried out;
» the skills and knowledge needed; and
» team dynamics.

Of course, there is no reason why a team should always remain the same size once it has been set up. Additions to it may be made on a permanent basis or on a temporary basis, either from within the organization or from outside it.

For example, Charles Handy (1989) talks about the "shamrock organization," in which, like the plant, there are three connected parts:

» the core workers – on full- or part-time salaries;
» contracted workers – on fixed-term contracts; and
» the flexible workforce – hired as required on a daily, weekly, or monthly basis.

In this type of organization, teams might be made up of a majority of core workers, with contractors and flexible workers brought in as and when their specific skills are required.

When the membership of a team changes, through people joining, leaving, or both, this can have a significant effect upon the behavior of the people who form the new team.

TEAM EVOLUTION

Tuckman (1965) identified four stages of team evolution.

» **Forming** – when the team first meets together. At this stage, people are very wary of each other and reveal very little of themselves to others.
» **Storming** – when people begin to assert themselves and to vie for position. This inevitably leads to a certain amount of conflict.
» **Norming** – when the team settles down and begins to work more effectively.
» **Performing** – when the team performs to its very best and meets or exceeds its objectives.

Some teams move very quickly through the stages to become a very effective cohesive unit. Others may spend more time in the intermediate stages, and some never make it as far as the performing stage.

It is also possible to go back through the stages. We will look at this concept in more detail in Chapter 8.

Two further stages are possible but not inevitable.

» **Mourning** – this might be reached if a very valued member leaves the team for whatever reason. The remaining team members may feel depressed at their loss and this may affect their performance. They may even resent the newcomer who replaces the team member who has moved on, feeling that they will never be able to fill the void that has been left.
» **Adjourning** – this stage occurs when teams have finished the task for which they have been set up and simply disband. This may cause all of the team members to feel a sense of loss and they may take this forward to their new position.

Team leaders need to be aware of all of these stages so that action can be taken to support the team as it goes through a particular stage.

TRAINING AND DEVELOPMENT

We need to make a distinction here between *training* and *development*.

» **Training** is about giving people the knowledge, skills, and attitudes to carry out their current role.
» **Development** is about preparing them for future roles or changes to their current role.

We mentioned, in the previous chapter, the importance of investing time and effort in training and developing teams as well as individuals. To help us identify the difference between *individual* training and development and *team* training and development, we can return to the field of sport and take a further analogy from the game of soccer.

It is clearly very important that each *individual* player practices and develops their own skills of:

» ball control;
» tackling;
» making crucial passes to team mates;
» taking penalties; and
» scoring goals.

However, it is perhaps even more vital that, as a *team*, they develop:

» an awareness of each player's role in the team;
» an understanding of each member's strengths and weaknesses;
» a system of playing together (tactics) that will outmaneuver the opposing team;
» a plan to atone for any errors that any individual may make;
» flexibility to change the system if it isn't working;
» a team spirit to ensure that it is motivated at all times; and
» an understanding of precisely what the team is trying to achieve.

These skills are likely to allow a collection of talented individuals to grow into an effective team.

The same principles apply in exactly the same way in the business world. Working as a team, people will be able to employ their own individual skills to help the team as a whole to meet the overall objectives of the business.

Q: So how do we know what training or development a team needs?

A: We need to carry out a training needs analysis.

Many organizations use a competency framework. This identifies the range of knowledge, skills, and attitudes that will need to be demonstrated by individuals or teams if their objectives are going to be met.

Through a system of feedback and regular appraisal meetings, it is possible to see how effectively people are demonstrating these skills. Areas for further development can be agreed. In this way, any gap between what needs to be achieved and what is actually being achieved can be identified. This is usually referred to as the "training gap."

We also need to look forward to see what additional knowledge, skills, and attitudes the team may need for any future roles. Any gaps identified here might be regarded as the "development gap." Once a gap is identified, action needs to be taken to satisfy the training or development need.

Methods of training and development

There may be many methods that can be used to satisfy a particular training or development need, as we shall see below. The most appropriate methods should be agreed with the team and a plan should be put in place to ensure that the training takes place.

Team training and development methods include:

» activity learning;
» role plays/simulations;
» case studies;
» group discussions;
» learning support groups;
» projects and work assignments.

In addition, individuals within the team may need training and development in particular areas. Methods include:

» lectures or presentations;
» mentoring, coaching, or giving instruction;
» individual research or individual practice;
» videos, tapes, or CD-ROMs;
» job shadowing, secondments, job swaps, or networking.

In Chapter 6 we will focus in more detail on the team training methods and analyze which may be most appropriate in which situations.

KEY LEARNING POINTS

» A team needs a common purpose.
» This should be translated into SMART objectives.
» There are various types of team.
» Teams need to be organized into effective structures.
» Teams expect certain qualities from their leader.
» Teams go through several stages as they develop.
» Developing teams is as important as developing individuals.
» There are a variety of methods of developing teams.

The Evolution Of Developing Teams

This chapter gives an analysis of how the concepts have evolved. It includes discussions on:

- » ''Human Relation'' theories;
- » motivation;
- » quality;
- » team dynamics;
- » team cultures;
- » team leadership;
- » team roles;
- » the pool/squad approach; and
- » coaching within teams.

The use of teams can be traced way back in history, particularly in military and political spheres. Armies have traditionally fought in clearly defined teams, with the Romans being an especially famous example, with their well-organized legions made up of teams of 100 men under the leadership of a centurion.

Skipping forward to the early part of the twentieth century, the period began with a focus on "scientific management," as pioneered by F.W. Taylor (1856–1915). This involved working out the best method by which an individual might carry out a task and recording the time it took to do it. It was very much involved with the processes of work rather than the people doing the work.

It was in the late 1920s that Elton Mayo (1880–1949) began to look at the human relationships involved in the workplace. It soon became clear that the way in which people interacted with each other was an important factor in their effectiveness at work.

In the mid-twentieth century a lot of work was carried out on motivating people to work more effectively, particularly in teams. Studies were made about the way teams evolved, how they were composed, how they were led, and the varying ways in which different teams worked together. At the same time the drive towards total quality management (TQM) led to the development of quality circles.

Towards the end of the century, there was a focus on how team performance could be improved, and many organizations began programs of team building and coaching. The 1980s saw another interesting development: the pool or squad system, in which people are part of a team and are available to it, but are not always called upon to play a part.

TIMELINE

The following timeline shows the evolution of academic thought on team development.

» **1920s**: "Human relations" theories
» **1940s**: Motivation
» **1950s**: Quality circles

» **1960s**: Team dynamics
» **1970s**: Team cultures and team leadership
» **1980s**: Team roles and the pool/squad approach
» **1990s**: Coaching within teams

We can now look at each of these in more detail.

"HUMAN RELATIONS" THEORIES

Elton Mayo (1880-1949) carried out a series of experiments between 1924 and 1932 at the former Hawthorne Works of the Western Electric Company, which later became AT&T.

Particularly relevant to our study of team development were the following experiments.

1927–32 relay–assembly test room experiments

A number of women were separated from the other workers into a team. Changes were made to their working arrangements; they were allowed an input into the changes each time and generally worked as an autonomous group without a supervisor. They covered for each other if someone was below par and they met socially outside work. Their productivity increased.

This series of experiments demonstrated that the productivity of the workforce was affected by a number of factors, including:

» the amount of responsibility people have;
» to what extent they can organize their own work;
» social interaction with other workers; and
» how they are supervised.

1931–32 bank wiring observation room experiments

A number of men were removed from their usual workplace and formed into a group in a separate test room. No changes were made to their working arrangements. They were simply observed and interviewed. It became clear that the group had a clear idea of what a fair day's work looked like and would put pressure on anyone who produced more or less, with the result that group production norms were maintained. They also protected the group, ensuring that no-one did or said anything that would harm any members of the group.

This series of experiments demonstrated that team members interact in a complex way and will establish their own informal rules for working together, in fact embracing a *team culture*. We will look more closely into team cultures later in this chapter.

MOTIVATION

Following Mayo, writers on management issues focused upon motivating staff in order to encourage them to work more effectively.

For example, the need to socialize with other people at work was seen by many writers as a motivating factor. Abraham Maslow (1943) suggested that there is a hierarchy of human needs and that as each more elaborate need is satisfied we are motivated by the next need in the hierarchy. Thus, we need food and water to keep us alive; once we have them, we need shelter to keep us safe. The third need in the hierarchy is the need for socialization with others. The fourth and fifth are esteem and self-actualization. (See Fig. 3.1.)

Fig. 3.1 Maslow's hierarchy of needs. Adapted from Abraham Maslow (1943) "A theory of human motivation." *Psychological Review*, **50** (No. 4).

Socialization and esteem, in particular, are clearly very relevant to working in teams. It suggests that the need to work with people whom we like and to be recognized by them as having done a good job are significant motivating factors.

Frederick Herzberg (1966) suggested that there were two key sets of factors: motivators and hygiene factors.

Motivators would actually motivate people:

» achievement;
» responsibility;
» recognition;
» the work itself;
» advancement.

Hygiene factors would not necessarily motivate people, but would certainly cause dissatisfaction if they were not adequately provided:

» interpersonal relations;
» how people are supervised;
» company policy;
» salary;
» working conditions.

All of these factors are very relevant when we consider how we might develop teams. McClelland (1961) suggests that people have needs for:

» achievement;
» affiliation;
» power.

According to this theory, these needs develop over time and only one tends to motivate at any given time.

Throughout motivation theory the needs for interaction, achievement, esteem, and power over one's own work are continually recurrent themes. In Chapter 6 we will look in more detail at how these concepts might be used to develop more effective teams in practice.

QUALITY CIRCLES

In the middle of the twentieth century there was a focus on quality and several very influential figures emerged to persuade organizations to adopt the techniques of total quality management (TQM). Kaoru Ishikawa (1972) was very influential concerning the introduction of quality circles, which became very popular in Japanese industry, especially in the large manufacturing companies such as Nissan and Toyota, though they did not enjoy such great popularity elsewhere in the world.

A quality circle is made up of representatives from several different functions of the organization, who meet regularly to discuss quality issues and, even more importantly, to come up with solutions. They are a good example of a secondary team, which we met in Chapter 2, as they do not work closely together in their normal working duties.

TEAM DYNAMICS

In Chapter 2 we saw that, during the 1960s, B.W. Tuckman identified the stages through which most teams will pass on their way to becoming effective. At the same time, other theorists began to analyze how individuals behave when they are members of a team.

B.M. Gross in *Organizations and their Managing* (1968), for example, set out a list of the types of people who are likely to be found in a team. Their various types of behavior are summarized by Andrew Kakabadse *et al.* in *Working in Organizations* (1988).

Generally, the theorists identified three main types of team behavior.

1. **Task-oriented behavior**, which helps to complete the team's task, such as:

   » proposing ideas and courses of action;
   » building upon other people's ideas;
   » seeking information from members of the team;
   » giving information to the team;
   » seeking other opinions;
   » offering different opinions/alternative suggestions in an assertive, rather than aggressive manner;
   » checking understanding, both one's own and other people's; and
   » summarizing the situation at regular intervals.

2. **Team/maintenance-oriented behavior**, which helps to maintain harmony in the team, such as:

   » encouraging others to put forward their ideas;
   » using humor to diffuse a tense situation;
   » creating a climate in which people can be open with one another;
   » being friendly and warm to others;
   » using open body language; and
   » seeking compromise and harmony at times of potential conflict.

3. **Power/self-oriented behavior**, which is aimed at increasing a particular member's own status or power, such as:

   » attacking other people's ideas;
   » rejecting ideas without allowing full discussion;
   » blocking proposals without giving alternatives;
   » finding fault with every idea;
   » defending one's own ideas even when they are indefensible;
   » interrupting people when they are still putting forward their suggestions;
   » excluding people deliberately;
   » talking too much so other people aren't given the opportunity to contribute;
   » staying silent when not getting one's own way; and
   » diverting the discussion on to a more comfortable topic.

TEAM CULTURE

This interest in team dynamics led people to consider team culture. One of the best-known frameworks of organizational culture was put forward by R. Harrison (1972) and built upon by Charles Handy (1978). It identified four types of culture.

» **Power** – in which the key power figure sits at its center, like a spider spinning its web, pulling all the strings.
» **Role** – which tends to be hierarchical, with everyone having their own very specific job specifications and clearly identified responsibilities.

» **Task** – which is seen mainly in small project teams or close-knit departments of an organization, where a more flexible approach is needed.
» **Person** – which consists of a number of people who share facilities and systems, but who tend to operate on their own. Many professional organizations might have such a culture, such as dentists, doctors, or solicitors.

We will look at these four types of culture in more detail in Chapter 8.

Another well-known framework is that of Deal and Kennedy (1982), which plots two factors against one another:

» the degree of risk attached to the organization's activities; and
» the speed at which the organization receives feedback on how successful its strategies have been.

This produces four main types of organization.

» **High risk/quick feedback** – the tough-guy, macho culture, found in entrepreneurial organizations.
» **Low risk/quick feedback** – the work-hard, play-hard culture, found in highly energetic companies producing a variety of fast moving products.
» **High risk/slow feedback** – bet-your-company-culture, found in organizations where research takes a relatively long time to come to fruition.
» **Low risk/slow feedback** – process culture, which tends to exist in highly regulated organizations.

We will also look at these types of culture in more detail in Chapter 8.

Any organization may have several different types of cultures within it, in different departments or areas. For example, an airline department that deals with safety might be governed by a lot of procedures and regulation and may be a role culture; the same company's cabin crew working in the aircraft might adopt a task culture as the decisions they take on customer service are their own responsibility.

TEAM LEADERSHIP

There are a variety of theories about what makes a good leader and from the 1970s there was great interest in styles of leadership. Earlier, it had been thought that leaders were either born to leadership (like President J.F. Kennedy, for example) or blossomed through a particular event (like Winston Churchill in World War II).

In the 1970s, however, people began to look at what leadership really meant and which style of leadership brought the best results. There were several theorists of particular note.

Robert Tannenbaum and Warren H. Schmidt (1973) viewed leadership as a continuum, with at one end an authoritarian approach, in which the leader takes all of the decisions, and at the other, through a variety of consultative approaches, a democratic approach, where the team members make the decisions.

Robert R. Blake and Jane S. Mouton (1985) set out the "managerial grid," based on two main factors:

» concern for people; and
» concern for production.

This produces five main leadership styles.

» **High production/low people** – a very authoritarian style which takes little account of the needs of team members.
» **High people/low production** – a style which shows a high concern for the team and its members but may not focus on getting the job done.
» **Low team/low production** – a style which takes little interest in the team or its objectives.
» **Mid team/mid production** – a style which takes adequate account of team members and the task in hand; it may not be particularly effective, but it does recognize the requirement to balance the needs of the task and the team.
» **High production/high team** – a style which takes account of the objectives that need to be met and also of the needs of the team and its members. This style seeks to lead by agreement and motivation rather than by force.

Paul Hersey and Ken Blanchard (1977) suggested that the style used should be a response to the team members' needs and may need to be varied for each team member. We will look at this in more detail in Chapter 8.

John Adair (1979) suggests that a good leader will balance the three intertwining circles of:

» task – what needs to be achieved;
» individual – the needs of each team member; and
» team – the needs of the team as a whole.

We will look at this in more detail in Chapter 8.

TEAM ROLES

As we saw in Chapter 2, Meredith Belbin focused on the various natural roles of team members. He identified nine team roles:

» **co-ordinator** – who ensures that everyone's view is taken into account;
» **shaper** – who drives the team to complete the task;
» **team worker** – who keeps the team in harmony, minimizing conflict;
» **plant** – who provides new ideas;
» **monitor evaluator** – who ensures that all choices or options are considered;
» **implementer** – who turns ideas into action;
» **completer finisher** – who ensures that the task is completely finished off;
» **resource investigator** – who builds up contacts outside the team; and
» **expert** – who contributes deep knowledge on specific issues.

Each person would be predisposed towards one or more of these types as their primary team role. Members would also have secondary roles that they could perform if necessary. Belbin argued that all of these roles need to be represented if the team is to work effectively, though members could perform more than one role. Where roles are not performed adequately, the team will find itself at a disadvantage. We will look at this in more detail in Chapter 8.

THE POOL/SQUAD APPROACH

The pool or squad approach is often seen in sport, where each team may have a number of reserves and substitutes. In some cases a team will have two or more players who share or compete for a particular position. This provides cover in the case of injury to one or the other, but it also allows the team to have a variety of tactical options as different players are combined in different patterns.

This approach is also used in many other areas of life. For example, television soap operas usually have a set number of characters who will appear in any given episode. Some characters will not appear for weeks at a time, then may return for a nightly appearance for a few weeks. As one character returns, so another will take a rest. If a new character is introduced on a permanent basis, then usually one of the current characters is written out of the series.

We mentioned Charles Handy's "shamrock organization" in Chapter 2. This type of organization will often have a number of contractors whom they will use when needed. The company will check them out for service quality and maintain a list of approved contractors upon whom they can call as required. At any one time, they may use just a few of them. This is particularly common among training organizations, which, instead of (or as well as) employing their own trainers, will select from a pool of freelance trainers whom they know and trust as and when new training contracts are won. For the length of that contract the trainers will act as a team. As the contracts come to an end, the trainers will find themselves either working with a different team, or sitting this one out. In this way, the organization can exactly meet the fluctuating demand for its products as it arises, without the need to maintain a high level of permanent staff.

Many universities, for example, employ a core of permanent lecturers and call upon a pool of additional people on short-term contracts as they need them. Competition for selection ensures that all team members continue to develop their knowledge and skills to the highest quality levels.

COACHING WITHIN TEAMS

In the 1990s, organizations began to realize the great benefits that could result from coaching individuals, often on a one-to-one basis. Personal development plans, through which individuals could identify their needs for development and set out an action plan to fulfill them, became increasingly popular. It meant that good performers could be encouraged to produce even better results.

In the UK's financial services industry, which is regulated by the Financial Services Authority (FSA), team leaders are encouraged to spend time with each team member in a personal coaching session at least once every three months.

It has become very common now for team members with particular skills to coach other team members, rather than sending people away on courses. In this way, many of the skills in the team can be cascaded through it.

KEY LEARNING POINTS

The evolution of developing teams included the following concepts:

» "human relations" theories;
» motivation;
» quality circles;
» team dynamics;
» team cultures;
» team leadership;
» team roles;
» the pool/squad approach;
» coaching within teams.

The E-Dimension

The new technology of the twenty-first century offers new opportunities for developing teams. This chapter explores some of the latest tools, including:

» the Internet;
» intranets;
» extranets;
» e-mail;
» tracking systems;
» computer/video conferencing;
» chatrooms;
» bulletin boards and newsletters; and
» recruitment and selection Websites.

In this chapter, we will look at how e-technology helps teams to become more effective. We can analyze how e-technology makes it easier for team members to interact with each other and with their customers and suppliers.

THE INTERNET

Because it contains such vast amounts of information, the Internet can be an excellent resource for teams, who are able to seek advice and information from a wide variety of external organizations. This is particularly useful for supplementing the knowledge that the team already possesses. It also helps to keep them abreast of any new developments that are taking place in respect of:

» their own processes and operations;
» their competitors' products; and
» their suppliers' ability to offer them new products.

Such information can be used to help them to make more informed decisions and to consider new ideas.

There are also a great number of specialist sites where consultants can give advice on specific problems, which is invaluable when the team is troubleshooting.

The team can also set up its own Website, where it may offer to carry out services for customers who access it.

INTRANETS

An intranet is an Internet-like network that is maintained privately within an organization. The team can access a lot of information about what is going on in other parts of the organization, particularly in areas of:

» new policy;
» new strategy;
» performance against targets;
» new processes.

They will also be able to find out about other specific individuals and teams, to see what they are doing and how they are performing. An intranet can be a particularly invaluable tool during periods when an organization is undergoing significant changes.

Many successful organizations have set up their own internal libraries where they maintain reference and training materials. Some have even set up their own internal universities, for example, American Airlines at Fort Worth and McDonald's in Illinois in the US.

EXTRANETS

An extranet is a private system like an intranet, but is shared between trading organizations. It has the same advantages as an intranet, with the added bonus of providing access to what is happening in partner organizations.

Some organizations have links with their suppliers and customers so that traditional ordering and invoicing procedures do not become outdated. Instead, each organization in the supply chain will have access to information concerning its customer's stocks and potential sales of particular items. It can then supply the necessary items in good time before they are needed, without them needing to be ordered physically by the customer. Order forms and invoices are raised and sent through the system automatically as the order is supplied.

Unilever is one firm that has made use of extranets. We shall be looking at this organization in detail later in this chapter.

E-MAIL

The growth of e-mail since the early 1990s has been immense and global. Once people have used e-mail for a short period, they begin to wonder how they ever managed without it. It is very easy to use to exchange information quickly and often informally. It is particularly powerful for sending information between team members as the system can easily be set up to distribute messages to everyone in the team at the push of a button. Arranging team meetings, for example, is much simpler; possible dates can be sent out to everyone at once and replies can be received within minutes.

E-mail can also be used to keep the team in constant touch with customers and suppliers, helping to establish relationships with impor-tant contacts outside the team itself.

TRACKING SYSTEMS

Tracking systems are relatively new and allow a team to keep track of where individual team members are at any time, wherever they may be in the world.

Team members feed into the system their intended movements and update their itinerary as it rolls out, feeding in any changes that occur en route. In this way, they can be contacted in case of emergency or if any important issue comes up.

In addition, when team members are abroad, the system allows information to be passed to them about anything they may need to know before they arrive in a particular location, such as:

» entry requirements;
» health issues;
» transport arrangements;
» banking arrangements;
» key current local issues.

Apart from giving the person specific information that is useful to them, this also imparts a feeling of continuing support for someone who may be working a long way from the other members of the team.

Knowing the whereabouts of individuals may also allow the team to decide who is best placed to respond to a particular customer enquiry or to take on a particular project in the vicinity.

One example of a tracking system is iJet's WorldCueTraveler, which is currently expanding its coverage from 154 countries to an expected 180 in the near future. Organizations that use tracking systems include global concerns such as the World Bank, whose employees carry out more than 25,000 business trips per year.

Tracking systems can also be used to track training and development. We recognized, in Chapter 2, the need for a training needs analysis to be carried out for teams so that any additional training or development needs can be identified. Software programs, such as those provided by Work Smart, for example, allow the current level of skills and knowledge of the individual team members to be compared with the overall needs for the team, so that gaps are clearly visible.

It is also possible to look forward to see what the future requirements might be after, say, a change in legislation. As people are trained in the new skills/procedures a clear picture of the overall knowledge and skill levels available in the team can be built up. Links can be made to specific training packages on the Internet or organizational intranet.

COMPUTER OR VIDEO CONFERENCING

Computer or video conferencing allows the team to hold a virtual meeting even if some team members are far from their normal place of work.

In the early 1990s, it was widely held that video conferencing, in which two or more people can see and hear each other while remaining in different locations, would pose a major threat to the transport industry, as people carried out meetings from their offices rather than jumping on an airplane. However, a number of obstacles prevented it from growing as rapidly as its champions thought.

» Many people were afraid of new technology or of talking into the "black box."
» There was a belief among many that the quality was not very good, particularly for long-distance calls, where a time delay often confused the unwary.
» People liked to travel and did not want to lose what they saw as a perk.

By 2002, however, these obstacles had largely disappeared. Many more people began to embrace the new technology rather than being afraid of it; their familiarity with computer technology and web cams may well have helped. New high-speed data links meant that sound and picture quality became better than ever and delays were minimal. Many people now prefer not to travel, either because of the trauma over the events of September 11, 2001 in the US, or because they have begun to recognize how tiring, as opposed to glamorous, constant travel is.

There are two main types of arrangement:

» **Desktop to desktop** – the simplest and cheapest form and particularly appropriate for small teams. It involves installing video camera equipment, software, and a high-speed link between the computers concerned. Team members can then carry out a video conference from their work desks.

» **Conference suites** – these are becoming very popular. Some larger organizations may have their own video conference suite, while many hotels now offer video conferencing facilities. The arrangements make it appear that people are virtually in the same room, talking together.

Responding to the downturn in business travel in 2001, Marriott Hotels have already established 12 conference suites in their hotels throughout the UK and intend to introduce a further 27 in the very near future.

Apart from keeping the team in touch without requiring them to move far from their own desk, video conferencing brings significant cost savings, including:

» a reduction in downtime while the executives travel;
» no expenditure on travel tickets, motoring costs, taxis, or public transport costs; and
» fewer overnight hotels and hospitality costs.

In the year 2000–01 British Telecom saved some £6mn in the UK by using conferencing rather than traveling to meetings. Large multi-national organizations such as Unilever find video conferencing invaluable for transatlantic conferences linking the US, the UK and the Netherlands (see the case study later in this chapter).

It is also possible to incorporate software applications into the conferencing arrangements. This allows a presentation to be made to the virtual meeting, so that people can make proposals and presentations to the rest of the team, without the team actually having to meet up in person. Conferences can be recorded so that people who are unable to attend the real-time conference can catch up with what was discussed later on at a time convenient to them.

Video conferencing is also ideal for training or skills updates. Training sessions can also be arranged so that the trainer is at one location and the delegates are elsewhere. We will look at this in more detail in Chapter 5.

CHATROOMS

These Internet-, intranet-, or extranet-based facilities allow team members to discuss issues, concerns, or problems with other people inside or outside their organization in real time and in writing. This often enables the team to access useful insights, opinions, and information, which may help them to solve specific problems or clear obstacles. Discussions can be attended by a number of people, so that information can be exchanged very quickly.

Members of a team can set up chatrooms for their own use only, so that they can discuss concerns and issues with each other directly and in confidence.

BULLETIN BOARDS AND NEWSLETTERS

These are particularly useful to help the team to keep up-to-date about what is currently happening on a project. Bulletin board messages concerning specific issues are posted on a central Website and members can access them as required. Newsletters can be sent to all members of the team covering a whole range of current topics that may be of interest to them.

Some airlines use online briefings for flight crew and cabin crew to keep them abreast of the latest relevant information they may need for their flight.

The Chartered Insurance Institute has also started to provide, through its online library, a wide range of reports which are of interest to organizations in the financial services industry.

RECRUITMENT AND SELECTION WEBSITES

There are a large number of Websites available today on which people can post their CVs and seek jobs, and from which potential employers can sift through CVs to find people who could be useful to them as employees, contractors, or consultants.

Using the sites to find people who have the skills that the team needs, but currently does not have, will help to strengthen the team, either by bringing in a permanent team member in the long term or hiring a contractor for the short term. The team is able to consider a wide range of prospective candidates, including individuals who are geographically far away – e-technology may allow those people to make their contribution remotely from their own office, which may sometimes be their own home.

SOME PITFALLS FOR E-TEAMS

As we have seen, it is now possibly to work in virtual teams, with team members rarely, if ever, actually meeting each other, working together or even speaking to each other.

This does, however, have some implications for team cohesion. In previous chapters we have considered issues such as motivation, synergy, and team interaction and have seen how powerful these can be in improving team effectiveness. The danger with the virtual team is that these areas can easily be neglected, with the result that some of the real benefits of team working are lost.

So what can you do to ensure that the team grows into a cohesive unit? Here are some ideas.

» Take every opportunity to bring your people together as a team, for example for conferences, training, or social events.
» Encourage team members to use the telephone and video conferencing rather than relying solely on e-mail to communicate.
» Recommend that they have some face-to-face meetings with other team members.
» Use newsletters with photographs so that people can put at least some faces to names.
» Celebrate successes together whenever possible.

CASE STUDY: UNILEVER

Unilever is a global business, with some 300,000 employees with operations in nearly 90 countries. Its products are bought in some 150 countries worldwide. There are two main strands to its business and it is organized into two main global divisions:

» **Foods** – brands include Ragu, Lipton, Colman's, Bird's Eye, Frisko.
» **Home and personal care** – brands include Dove, Persil, Ponds, Omo.

Its corporate headquarters are in Rotterdam, in the Netherlands, and in London, UK.

Unilever has embraced e-technology wholeheartedly and it is found throughout many of the company's systems and processes. Here are some examples of the technology that Unilever uses to enhance the effectiveness of its teams.

» **Video conferencing** – Unilever has its own dedicated video conferencing suites and they are used so extensively at peak times that they can be fully booked; in this case the company will use adjacent hotel facilities, if they are available, like those offered by the Marriott Hotels chain mentioned earlier in this chapter. The company makes significant savings on travel and accommodation expenses using this approach. It also reduces the fatigue that can affect executives who travel continuously on business.

» **Internet and intranet** – the company is a great believer in using teams that communicate horizontally through the organization rather than using traditional hierarchical channels. It seeks to use the Internet to gain huge amounts of information, as well as to market its products.

However, Unilever recognizes the pitfalls of swamping everyone with e-mails which have no relevance to them, so that nobody has a chance to read them all. It considers itself to be an intelligent organization, which shares information in a systematic way, rather than simply sending e-mails to everyone about everything. Teams who need the information are able to access it easily.

In several countries, local teams have an intranet facility which means they can keep up to date with new development opportunities, the latest company initiatives, and strategic decisions.

As far as the supply chain is concerned, Unilever can access, through the Internet, a huge range of items from a wide range of sources at previously negotiated prices. However, they are looking towards setting up systems and processes so that the whole supply chain can be planned and forecast in collaboration with key suppliers and customers. Thus, teams in each part of the supply chain will find their work much easier and they will, at each stage of the chain, be able to satisfy more accurately their customers' requirements.

In addition to this, in several places, sales teams are equipped with small computers, which allow customer orders to be sent instantly on to the appropriate warehouse for immediate processing and distribution. Clearly, e-technology has permeated throughout this company.

KEY LEARNING POINTS

» The Internet enables teams to access vast amounts of information.

» Teams can keep in touch with organizational policy and strategy through an intranet.

» Extranets are very useful between trading partners.

» E-mail keeps teams in touch, though it needs to be used intelligently.

» Tracking systems can provide support for team members who are working away.

» Video conferencing can promote team building and reduce costs.

» Recruitment and selection Websites can be a useful source when the team needs additional skills.

» There are some possible pitfalls with e-technology that teams need to avoid.

The Global Dimension

This chapter looks at the application of the concepts of developing teams in the global marketplace, including:

» multi-cultural teams;
» maintaining performance;
» keeping in touch;
» distance learning; and
» a case study of Médecins Sans Frontières

In this chapter we will analyze the implications for teams that are working on a global scale. We saw, in Chapter 2, the importance of deciding how teams are to be structured within an organization. When that organization is operating in the global marketplace it becomes even more vital that care is taken when setting up teams.

MULTI-CULTURAL TEAMS

A global organization may set up teams in several formats:

» multi-cultural teams throughout the organization;
» different single-culture teams located in different parts of the organization; or
» a mix of multi- and single-culture teams.

This can become more complex when we take team leaders into account, as the head office may:

» send out its own people to lead teams which are composed of local people from the country concerned;
» send out its own teams which are led by a local person from the country concerned; or
» use local people to lead local teams.

Many organizations, such as Coca-Cola, for example, who have local operations in nearly 200 countries world-wide, prefer to "think local – act local" because it enables them to respond more effectively to their local customers' needs. Such organizations tend, therefore, to use mostly local staff as far as possible, though they may also have a number of expatriates.

Let's now have a look at some of the cultural differences that might apply in various parts of the world, because they may have an impact on the way team members interact with each other.

Most people seem to enjoy meeting people from different cultures and usually welcome the opportunity to work with them. Certainly this is true for the people who work for Médecins Sans Frontières, which provides the case study at the end of this chapter. Let's consider some of the real value which multi-cultural working brings.

» It allows the airing of different perspectives on problems.
» It can help in finding new solutions.
» It allows the making of new and different friends.
» It can help in learning a new language.
» It gives the chance to listen to different experiences.
» It allows for the sharing of complex problems.

Fons Trompenaars (1993) has carried out some very interesting research on different types of international culture. Some of his work has significant relevance for team development. His research suggests that people from different cultures would have different views on a variety of issues. (See Table 5.1.)

For example, in Japan, people tend to make little distinction between their public and their private selves, so, in order to build up a business relationship, you need to get to know the person. In the US, however, you can work quite happily with someone without knowing much about them personally.

Table 5.1

Some will:	Others will:
See the individual as most important	See the group as most important
Be concerned for upholding rules	Be more concerned for the people caught up in them
Show a lot of emotion	Show little emotion
Make little distinction between personal and public self	Keep them very separate
Accord people status because they have achieved it	Accord people status because their position entitles them to it
Regard the future as most important	Regard tradition as most important
Feel we should try to control nature	Feel we should let nature take its course

All of this has implications for multi-cultural teams. It is worth considering some examples of where potential conflict or misunderstanding might occur:

» In the US, the present and the future are considered most important, but in France there is a great sense of tradition, with the past being very important.
» In the UK, a leader is only respected if he or she earns that respect, while in Japan respect may come automatically with the position.
» In Singapore, rules tend to be very well respected, while in many other countries, they may be broken if there is a good enough reason.
» In some countries, such as those around the Mediterranean, people quite openly show emotion, while in others people remain expressionless, whatever they may be feeling.

Clearly, there are many opportunities for people to misunderstand how people in other cultures are reacting to them, so preparing multi-cultural teams by ensuring they receive training about cultural similarities and differences would appear to be very important.

Rolls-Royce, the famous aero-engine company, does just that. Its head office is in Derby, UK, but it has units located throughout the world, in North and South America, Europe, and Asia. It operates a cultural awareness program, based in France. It is not alone. British Airways is another example of a company that offers its staff training in cultural awareness.

We also need to take account of a number of other aspects of culture.

» **Symbols** – some cultures are very protective of their flags, military installations, or their monarchy. A remark about the monarchy in one country may bring a polite smile, while in another it might lead to prosecution.
» **Rituals** – many countries have different views on the working day; in hot countries, it is usual to close down in the early afternoon and to reopen in the cool of the evening, while in more temperate countries people will work through the whole afternoon and go home in the evening. There are also many different religious ceremonies, with the result that people worship (and thus work) at different times in different countries.

» **Myths** – each culture will have a tradition of stories and myths which are important to them.

MAINTAINING PERFORMANCE

We have recognized the importance of managing the performance of the team in Chapter 2 and we will look at it again in Chapter 10. However, here we need to set out some of the key performance issues that may arise with teams that are spread around the globe. This might also include those organizations such as shipping companies or airlines, who have crews working in teams away from central control for long or short periods.

Managing performance relates to:

» the agreement of objectives;
» the monitoring of performance against them;
» the provision of feedback; and
» action planning for improvement where it is needed.

It is possible to identify some of the problems that might occur in a globally dispersed team and consider some possible solutions (see Table 5.2).

KEEPING IN TOUCH

Communicating within a team is never easy, especially when people go out of the office, go on holiday, or take sickness absence. There are a number of other things that take members away from the team for a while. Communicating within a global team is even more difficult. However, luckily, there are a number of tools to help us.

We have looked at most of the available e-technology tools in Chapter 4 and all of them can be particularly helpful for a global team, with e-mail, intra- and extranets, tracking systems, and video conferencing being especially useful. We can now look at how they might be used to help the global team (see Table 5.3).

Of course, the face-to-face meeting with team members and the team leader is especially important in developing relationships within the team. Even if, owing to the distances involved, most meetings are carried out by video conferencing, a face-to-face meeting can be vital

Table 5.2

Team members may:	Likely problems:	Possible solutions:
Rarely or never meet each other	They don't feel part of the team; don't buy into the objectives	Arrange meetings; use video conferencing if necessary; give them more information about the global picture
Rarely meet their team leader	They feel abandoned and unsupported; they receive written feedback only, or no feedback; their performance drops	Make time to meet them on a regular basis, at least for feedback and review meetings
Work with totally different customers; work mainly with a different, local team	They feel more loyalty for their local team and customers than for their global team	Encourage more communication between team members, use chatrooms, bulletin boards, newsletters; arrange meetings if possible
Work with different systems	Essential communications on performance issues are not always received or sent	Work towards compatible systems; until then, ensure that communications are sent in various formats that people can access
Have different perspectives from the rest of the team	They don't agree or see the point of the objectives	Give them more information about the global picture; train and develop them as a team when possible
Speak different languages	Poor or no communication	Use translators; encourage members to learn a common language

Table 5.3

Tool	Helps the global team to:
The Internet	Share useful and relevant sites with each other to gain knowledge, especially in respect of local knowledge of areas in which team members are located
Intranets	Keep abreast of company news and events
Extranets	Keep abreast of news and communicate with close trading partners, wherever in the world they may be
E-mail	Communicate with each other simply and directly, ensuring everyone receives the same message; allowing meetings to be arranged more simply
Tracking systems	Make arrangements to meet people in the team whenever they are nearby
Computer/video conferencing	Have a virtual meeting, which may be very important for building personal relationships
Chatrooms	Solve problems together and chat through specific issues
Bulletin boards, newsletters	Keep in touch with what is going on throughout the organization and within the team itself
Recruitment and selection Websites	Find local people to help when they need specific knowledge or skills that aren't already available within the team

at important points in a project or during a sales campaign to provide that extra bit of motivation and team spirit.

DISTANCE LEARNING

Distance learning programs are very important in the global context. Essentially, they allow people to learn and develop their skills while still doing their job at their own location. One of the most common approaches is a program of several people from throughout the organization working through a set of learning activities at the same time. Usually there will be a workbook on the topic, which can be delivered electronically through e-mail or through the company intranet. Workbooks are supported by trainers who are available to give advice to people over the telephone or through e-mail.

Particularly powerful programs also include seminars that the trainees can attend, where they meet their trainer and discuss issues. Progress through the program is usually through a series of work assignments or projects and the trainer gives feedback to individual delegates. Seminars can be used to discuss particular topics or carry out role plays.

Often, individuals, whether from the same team or not, will form learning support groups, which we look at in Chapter 6. People participating in a distance learning program often form networking groups of friends as a result of working together on the learning activities, and often they may remain close for many years despite their scattered physical locations and lack of face-to-face contact.

For a global team, distance learning can be an excellent solution because it allows the team to:

» train together so they are talking about the same issues and how it relates to their part of the business and their own objectives;
» meet each other regularly;
» interact with each other on business issues;
» meet socially afterwards;
» learn about other areas of the organization.

It is also possible to use video conferencing so that a trainer can facilitate remotely.

Training people together in this way will help to instill team spirit into a team that is dispersed across the globe.

CASE STUDY: MÉDECINS SANS FRONTIÈRES

Médecins Sans Frontières (MSF) is a private international humanitarian aid organization, which provides emergency medical assistance to populations in danger. It was set up in 1971 and deservedly won the Nobel Peace Prize in 1999 for its work around the world in helping those unable to help themselves.

Its mission statement contains two main strands:

» providing medical aid for any population anywhere that it is needed; and
» raising awareness of the situation of the people concerned.

The organization comes to the aid of populations wherever there is suffering, whether it be caused by war, famine, disease, earthquake, or other natural or man-made disaster. It is active in more than 80 countries worldwide and has over 2500 volunteers, who work together in teams alongside people from the local population of the country in which they are working. On average, there are seven local workers for every MSF expatriate volunteer.

Functional roles are mainly in the areas of:

» professional medical staff – doctors, nurses and other specialist medical staff who may be needed;
» logisticians – who work on transport, supplies, and engineering projects such as communications, buildings, sanitation, and water supplies; and
» financial administrators – who control the finance and budget for the project.

A typical team might be composed of several volunteers, each of a different nationality, working together with local people. An average posting for a volunteer is about six months, though this can sometimes be extended. In many of the countries in which they work, traveling is not easy, either because of the terrain or the political situation, and living conditions can be very difficult, including, in some locations, the possibility of disease.

Volunteers are clearly very motivated to do the job that they do. They are not paid, though their living expenses and fares are covered, so it is clear that they are not motivated by money. We can perhaps look more towards the following factors.

» **Achievement** – the volunteers clearly feel very deeply about helping others who are facing great hardship. Accounts of particular incidents that can be found on the organization's Website tell of the sense of achievement when their work is rewarded by success at saving the lives of people who might otherwise have died.
» **Responsibility** – other accounts tell of the need to make critical decisions in the field, using the skills within the team, though they can and do call upon higher authority when additional resources or high-level policy decisions are needed. They appear to provide good examples of task cultures in operation; that is, a group of highly skilled people working together towards a common goal, supporting each other towards the achievement of the goal, and making the necessary decisions quickly.
» **Social interaction** – team members also gain satisfaction from working together with people from other cultures and nationalities.
» **The work itself** – the work is often complex, challenging, and demanding.

Clearly, the teams who work for the organization are very dedicated to carrying out a challenging job in difficult circumstances.

KEY LEARNING POINTS

» Many organizations find multi-cultural teams add a lot of value to their business.
» People from different cultures may react in different ways.
» It is important to recognize the similarities and the differences between different cultures.
» Special care needs to be taken to maintain the high performance of global teams.
» E-technology is particularly useful for global teams to keep in touch.
» Distance learning can be an effective development tool for global teams.

Developing Teams: The State of the Art

This chapter examines the key debates, including:

- » the role of the team in embracing change;
- » enhancing team motivation;
- » methods of developing teams;
- » being an effective team member;
- » when teams get it wrong; and
- » when to empower, enable, or withhold power.

THE ROLE OF THE TEAM IN EMBRACING CHANGE

Change is a bit like inflation. When people say inflation is falling, they usually mean that the rate of increase is slowing down. So it is with change; it is always happening, it's only the rate at which it happens that fluctuates.

Over the last half-century, the pace of change has increased rapidly and it is showing no sign of slowing down. Many people who are working today will have seen immense changes in their lifetime, some of them altering the world only for the better. Despite this, people still *fear* change.

It is interesting that many people think that change is about losing something rather than gaining something better. We are often more comfortable with the current situation; even if it isn't very good, we would rather maintain it than risk something new. "Better the devil you know," as they say.

Kotter, Schlesinger, and Sathe (1986) identified four common reasons why people resist change.

» **Self-interest** – we are afraid that we might be worse off as a result of the change.
» **Lack of trust leading to misunderstanding** – previous experience may lead us to think that there is some ulterior motive behind the change or that we're not being told the full picture.
» **Different perspectives on the benefits** – a benefit to one person may appear a disadvantage to another; for example, changing the way a task is performed may make it simpler and cheaper to carry out, but it may also remove any challenge for the operator so that it becomes boring.
» **Low tolerance for change** – especially if there is constant change, and especially if the changes have not appeared to be particularly beneficial.

Teams can be a strong force in bringing about change. They can be equally powerful in resisting it. Table 6.1 shows how the team may react to four reasons either to drive or resist change.

Table 6.1

Reason	Team drives change	Team resists change
Self-interest	Members recognize team rather than individual interests and push for opportunities for the team	Team recognizes that each member shares a similar self-interest; digs in to resist
Lack of trust leading to misunderstanding	Not everyone has a reason to mistrust the proposals; they argue to give them a chance	Everyone mistrusts proposals; team forms solid resistance to fight them at all costs
Different perspectives on the benefits	Several members of the team can see potential benefits and argue for acceptance	Different individuals see various disadvantages and argue for resistance
Low tolerance for change	Positive team members argue that "this time it will be different, we can make the proposals work"	Resistant members argue, "it will never work, because we won't let it work"

As can be seen from Table 6.1, there are three main scenarios:

» the team goes for change – likely to be a positive force to embrace it;
» the team members argue for or against change – a critical mass will eventually emerge in favor of either embracing or resisting the change; or
» the team resists change wholeheartedly – likely to be a highly resistant force.

So how do we gain buy-in for change from the team? Table 6.2 lists some possible do's and don'ts.

Generally, the more the team is involved in the change process, the more likely it is to accept it or even push for it.

Table 6.2

Do	Don't
» Provide the team with the information they need so that they can work out for themselves that it is in their interests as a team that the change takes place.	» Withhold information so that the team is fed simply what you want it to know at any given time; they will see this as manipulation and resent it.
» Try to give the team ownership of some elements of the change so that they feel they have some control over what is happening.	» Impose the whole change on the team without giving them some input.
» Take account of their concerns; work with them to try to find ways of reducing their fears.	» Ignore or dismiss their genuine anxieties, because they are real.
» Be as open and honest with the team as possible; this may help to prevent mistrust and misunderstanding.	» Create a climate of "us and them, of "winners and losers."
» Acknowledge past mistakes and work with the team to find ways of avoiding them this time.	» Suggest that the last change only failed because the team prevented it from working.

Organizations that manage change effectively often find that their most successful teams actually put pressure on the rest of the organization to introduce change more quickly.

ENHANCING TEAM MOTIVATION

We saw in Chapter 3 that there are a number of theories of motivation. Many of them emphasize the importance of social interaction as a motivating factor.

Here we look specifically at how we might motivate a team to want to perform more effectively. Certainly, team members may still need to be motivated individually, because each person is different. Indeed, working in the team may be enough to motivate, for a while, some individual team members, who are currently at the "social" level of

Maslow's hierarchy of needs (see Chapter 3). An effective team leader will get to know individual team members so that they can find out what they respond to best.

Here are some examples of team motivation that are in common use across a wide range of organizations.

» Giving tangible rewards, such as money, vouchers, or sales conferences.
» Allowing the team more control over its workload.
» Handing the team more responsibility and authority.
» Agreeing realistic objectives/targets.
» Providing the tools and equipment they need.
» Encouraging competition between teams.
» Making the work itself interesting.
» Challenging competitors' teams directly.
» Allocating the next project.
» Giving praise for a job well done.

We can look at each of these in turn.

Giving tangible rewards, such as money, vouchers or sales conferences

These types of reward can be very effective in motivating people. To some people money is very important and they will work harder and more effectively to earn it. We saw in Chapter 3 that Herzberg included it in his "hygiene" factors rather than as a "motivator," so clearly not everyone agrees on the importance of monetary reward. What is clear from most theories is that people will be dissatisfied if they don't feel they are adequately rewarded. Often people only feel inadequately paid when they find out that someone else is earning more money than they are and it is possible that this is a status/self-esteem issue rather than a money issue in itself.

In many organizations it is difficult to give an additional monetary reward, because it interferes with salary bands, has tax implications for the individual, and may have a knock-on effect throughout a large set-up.

Some organizations link additional bonuses to specific achievements such as sales turnover or to the winning of specific contracts. Others choose to award holidays or gift vouchers.

One of the key difficulties here is that the team who receives the reward may have been ably assisted by other teams or individuals without whom they could not have met their bonus targets, yet rewards are often confined to the immediate team. This sometimes causes resentment.

Allowing the team more control over its workload

Maslow suggested that the highest level of his hierarchy of needs is "self-actualization," in which people have much more control about how they work and what they do. Teams that are allowed to organize their own working hours, working arrangements, and how they allocate work within the team tend to be very motivated.

Handing the team more responsibility and authority

Allowing the team to make its own decisions and take responsibility for them can be very motivating. Herzberg certainly saw it as a "motivator." Having to refer even the most minor decisions upwards can be very demotivating. We will look at this issue in more detail towards the end of this chapter.

Agreeing realistic objectives/targets

We saw the importance of SMART objectives in Chapter 2. A key factor is that they must be realistic ones that the team can achieve. If the team members feel that they are unattainable it is most likely that they will give up and not bother even to try. The objectives must also be challenging so that people have to make an effort to achieve them. The more challenging the work is, the more it stretches people and the greater the sense of achievement when it is completed.

Providing the tools and equipment they need

If the team is to do its best job, it needs the best tools. If this isn't possible, then it needs the best the organization can afford. Working with outdated and inefficient tools and equipment can be very dispiriting, especially if competitors have all the latest systems and equipment.

Encouraging competition between teams

Healthy competition can be very stimulating, so, if there are several similar teams in the organization, running competitions between them can be fun.

However, care needs to be taken that teams who don't often win don't become demotivated, or it will defeat the object. This can be managed by changing the criteria from time to time so that it brings into play a variety of skills and strengths.

Making the work itself interesting

The work should be challenging, as mentioned above. It should also be made as interesting as possible.

There are two main ways of making the work more interesting:

» **job enrichment** – giving people more responsibility; and
» **job enlargement** – widening the scope of the job so that it becomes more complex.

Sometimes it is possible to do both.

In 1990, the Swedish motor car manufacturer Volvo changed from a line process, in which people repetitively carried out a single task, to one in which a team built virtually a whole car. There was a marked increase in motivation and in the quality of the car that reached the customer.

Challenging competitors' teams directly

It can be an exhilarating moment of high achievement when the team learns that it has won a contract in the face of fierce competition.

Allocating the next project

Lining up the team for the next big or important task that is coming along can be a very powerful factor as it recognizes its efforts; it also gives the team members a feeling of security as it secures their workload for the immediate future.

Giving praise for a job well done

Giving praise for a job well done doesn't cost the organization anything. The more specific the praise regarding the importance of the team's achievement to the organization, the more motivating it will be.

Some organizations will write up specific successes in their newsletter so that the team receives wide acclaim. This will certainly help to increase the team members' self-esteem and make them feel recognized – both of which are identified by theorists as important elements of motivation.

With all of these possibilities, however, it is important to bear Victor H. Vroom's expectancy theory (1964) in mind. He suggests that people will work harder if they feel that it will lead to a particular reward that they value. If they feel it will not lead to the reward or that it will lead to a reward they do not value, then they are unlikely to work harder.

For example, if a team is promised book tokens if they meet their objective, they will only work hard if 1) they really believe that they will receive the book tokens and 2) they like reading and thus find the reward enticing. However, if they don't like reading and they don't value the reward, or don't believe it will be forthcoming, then they won't work any harder. If some of the team value the reward and others do not, then some will be motivated and the others will not.

So, even with team rewards, there is no substitute for getting to know the individuals in the team to ensure that the methods you are using are appropriate for them.

Threats to the team

One other aspect of team motivation needs to be considered here, because it can be very powerful. That is: **real or perceived threats to the team**.

Team members will usually rally round if they feel they are threatened in any way. The threat could take the form of a physically dangerous situation that the team finds itself in, like an emergency, a hostile takeover, or serious competition from other companies in one of the team's most important product areas.

METHODS OF DEVELOPING TEAMS

We saw in Chapter 2 that there are a number of methods that can be used to train and develop teams. Here we look at some that are specifically designed for teams rather than individuals, though it is certain that each person within the team will also need their own individual development plan to enhance their individual knowledge and skills.

We can look at the following in more detail:

» activity learning;
» role plays/simulations;
» case studies;
» group discussions;
» learning support groups; and
» projects and work assignments.

Before we look at each of these in turn, we need to consider the learning cycle and learning styles as they will affect which methods individual team members prefer.

The learning cycle

David Kolb (1979) identified four stages of the learning cycle. We can paraphrase them as follows:

» experiencing something;
» reflecting on what happened;
» analyzing why it happened and in what circumstances it might happen again; and
» testing out what might happen in different situations.

Different people will have a preference for the point at which where they enter the cycle. Peter Honey and Alan Mumford (1986) identified four learning styles that reflected these stages.

» **Activist** – likes to experience; jumps straight into an activity.
» **Reflector** – likes to reflect; needs time to think about what happened.
» **Theorist** – likes to analyze; develops theories about why it happened.
» **Pragmatist** – likes experimenting; tries out a different approach.

It is important to recognize that a team may contain people who have different learning styles and who may respond to learning opportunities in different ways.

Let's now look at some of the various methods.

Activity learning

In the latter part of the twentieth century, as team building began to grow in importance, activity events became quite popular. They are still widely used.

Usually, organizations send a team (or teams) of people to a location, where they spend a few days together. They perform a series of activities and learn by going through all of the four stages of the learning cycle together. Common activities include:

» orienteering;
» outdoor activities such as rock climbing/pot-holing/rafting;
» building machines;
» putting on plays;
» making films; or
» mock battles.

The common thread in these activities is that they:

» require a number of people;
» involve the achievement of a tangible end product;
» allow the opportunity to agree SMART objectives;
» need people to take on various roles or tasks;
» need a variety of skills if the team is to be successful;
» involve interaction between team members;
» need a number of decisions to be made by the team;
» require team members to rely on each other and possibly on other teams; and
» have a potential to lead to interpersonal conflict.

Usually the event will unfold in a series of activities involving all stages of the learning cycle and giving opportunities for all of the learning styles as it rolls out. For example:

» plan and carry out the first part of the activity;
» pause to review what went well and what did not;
» consider the implications of this for the next part of the activity;

» adjust their plans to take into account what they have learned;
» carry out the next stage of the activity;
» . . . and so on until the end of the event.

We could sum the process up as shown in Figure 6.1.

Fig. 6.1 The activity learning cycle.

Different people in the team will enjoy the various phases more or less according to their preferred learning style.

During the process, it is likely that the team members will come to rely on each other while undergoing some difficult situations. They may move through Tuckman's (1965) four stages of team evolution in the process. Often they will develop a bond and a team spirit which they can take back with them when they return to their workplace. They will also have practiced a wide range of team member and leadership skills.

Role plays/simulations

Role plays and simulations allow people to take part in an activity in a safe environment where they can try things out and there are no repercussions on the organization or its customers if things don't go according to plan. They are very useful for practicing activities such as:

» interviewing customers;
» handling customers with problems;
» giving and receiving feedback;
» leading meetings;
» handling negotiations; and
» recruitment and selection.

Scenarios can be practiced, and experienced coaches and/or the rest of the team can review performance, identifying any improvements that could be made.

Role plays are often criticized because they are "not the real thing," but they are, nevertheless, very useful in giving people confidence in handling a situation if they meet it in reality in their job. Team role plays also enable the team to gain experience of working with each other, so that they begin to know how another team member may react in a particular situation.

Simulations, in purpose-built electronic simulators, are used to enable flight crews and air traffic controllers to experience flying and controlling aircraft in both normal and emergency situations. They add huge value to the development of the crews because they allow them to practice emergency situations so that they are more likely to be able to deal with them effectively should they occur in reality. Many of these situations could not be practiced on a real flight because they might endanger the aircraft and passengers involved.

Simulation was a particularly important factor in the Shuttle-Mir space station program, which we will be looking at in more detail in Chapter 7.

Role plays tend to be preferred by activists, who like to be involved in the activity and are often disliked by reflectors, who prefer to observe and review what has happened rather than act out the role play themselves.

Case studies

Case studies allow a team to discuss what actions they might take in a particular situation, or to review an actual case that may have happened and to analyze how it might have been handled differently.

They are particularly useful for practicing problem solving and for identifying specific actions that might be taken in future to respond to customers. They allow different team members to advance their views and put forward their arguments. They are good for stimulating group discussion. Team members may learn a lot about each other's perspectives and values.

Team discussions

Team discussions about various issues allow team members to air their views. They can cover any topic, including systems and processes, or even performance.

They are particularly useful for ensuring that the whole team takes ownership of its activities and responsibilities, as they allow individual team members to bring up any points of concern so that they can be addressed.

Learning support groups

Learning support groups are relatively new to the development scene. They involve a group of workers who are improving their knowledge and skills as a part of either a company-wide development program or a program provided by an outside body such as a university or a training company. It might lead to the people achieving a qualification such as a diploma, or it may simply be an internal organizational program.

It is possible, if there is a wide geographical spread, that the people on the program may meet only rarely or even not at all. Under these conditions, it can often be difficult for individuals to find the determination or motivation to continue the program, especially if it becomes difficult and they find it tough going.

By setting up a learning support group, in which everyone on the program keeps in touch regularly for support, exchange of information or just for a chat, people are more likely to stay with the program. Simply knowing that there are other people out there undergoing the same learning process as they are gives people the strength and commitment to go on.

This is a very good example of team synergy, in that, as a team, most will stay the course. If they are working as individuals, some may well give up the program.

Projects and work assignments

Projects and work assignments have the outstanding feature that they allow the team to develop while still contributing to the overall team task or objective. They allow team members to get to know one another through working together. If decision making on the project is passed down to team members, the team can become used to making its own decisions, taking responsibility, and exercising authority.

Evaluation of training and development

Whatever method of training or development is used, it should have a purpose and should be capable of being evaluated to see whether it has been successful. Donald L. Kirkpatrick (1998) suggests that training should be evaluated on four levels.

» **Reaction** – how does the team feel during and immediately after the training? Was it worthwhile?
» **Learning** – to what extent have they improved their knowledge, skills, and attitudes?
» **Performance** – what behaviors are the team now demonstrating that they weren't demonstrating before the training?
» **Organizational results** – what additional value is the team now delivering for the organization? Could other teams benefit from the training? Could this team cascade the learning to them?

WHEN TEAMS GET IT WRONG

We have seen some good examples of how teams can add value in the workplace and we will see some more examples in Chapter 7. At this point, however, it might be useful to consider some of the instances when teams get it wrong. Here are three specific phenomena which can occur in some teams:

» group-think;
» risky shift;
» compromise.

Group-think

Group-think will usually occur within successful teams; in fact, it is usually caused by their very success.

The team begins to feel that it is invincible. Team members become convinced that all of their decisions are right. They also feel that they have the monopoly on being right and that no other opinions from outside the team count as much as their own. So they discount those opinions. If information comes to hand from outside the team that might throw doubt on their course of action, they will ignore it. If they find such information themselves, they will reinterpret it so that it does fit in with their decisions.

Members of the group who may have thought that the decision might be wrong and that there might be a better alternative will fall in line and conform with the majority; in any case, they would be ignored if they did not.

In this way, the team rushes headlong into disaster!

Teams that are lacking Belbin's (1981) natural team role of "monitor evaluator" (who ensures that all options are explored) or "co-ordinator" (who ensures everyone has the opportunity to give their opinion) may be particularly prone to group-think.

Risky shift

It is usually thought that it is less risky if a team takes a decision rather than a single person, because the team has a wider range of experience and knowledge to draw upon. Thus, if all opinions and ideas are properly heard and considered, the team will minimize the risk of being wrong.

Risky shift occurs when the team actually takes a more risky decision than any members would have taken if they had been making the decision themselves. Thus, as an individual, they might feel that authorizing $1mn on a piece of office equipment is excessive and might simply decide not to authorize it because it is too much. On the other hand, as a member of a team, they may well support the proposal, because the responsibility is not theirs alone and other people seem to think the equipment is both good value and vital to the operation. In fact, there may even be a majority of feelings in the team that the proposal should be turned down, but everyone supports it none the less, and it goes ahead.

Compromise

One of the dangers of working in a team is that everyone has a different view and decisions are watered down to the lowest form in a compromise to which everyone can agree. This can have two results:

» no-one in the team ends up with the solution that they wanted; or
» the actual solution is supported by no-one in the team.

In a dynamic, constantly changing environment, this can lead to the team being left behind by its competitors, who may have taken a bolder decision.

Compromise can be useful, though, especially when:

» no agreement is being reached and a temporary decision can be made;
» the advantages of achieving everything that people want are outweighed by the disadvantages, so that the gains are not worthwhile in the long run; or
» opinion is polarized round two opposing camps of similar power.

BEING AN EFFECTIVE TEAM MEMBER

If we are members of a team, what particular responsibilities do we have?

We have already seen that we:

» have to deliver our contribution towards the team objectives by carrying out our functional role;
» may have one or more natural team roles that we need to perform; or
» may, depending upon the style of leadership, have to obey the leader's or team's decisions.

But what else can we do, in our interactions with other members of the team, to ensure that everything runs smoothly?

Some teams agree amongst themselves a "team charter," which sets out some guidelines about how team members will interact with each other. A typical charter might suggest that team members:

» are honest with each other, especially with regard to feedback;
» are prepared to share information;
» respect each other's beliefs even if they don't agree;
» are open about how they feel;
» take turns with any chores;
» keep team issues confidential;
» are prepared to challenge ideas with which they don't agree; and
» embrace change as an opportunity.

Charters can be especially useful when a team is going through a period of storming, because they help to minimize conflict.

There is one further dimension to being an effective team member. This is **your individual role** – the role you play because you are you.

To what extent should we subordinate our own individuality on behalf of the team? And to what extent should we let it come out?

For one view on these questions we can look to the airline industry.

Richard Branson, chairman of Virgin Atlantic, feels that his customers like to see the human side of his company, so he encourages his staff to bring their personality to work with them. Interestingly, one of Virgin's main competitors, British Airways, followed this idea and urged its their cabin crew to display individuality too.

People with whom the team interacts – customers, suppliers, or other teams within the organization – are likely to respond to individuals with a name and a personality.

Working for multiple teams

Before we leave the various roles of a team member, we need to recognize that some people are members of several teams at the same time. Certainly, contractors may work with different people on each contract and they may have several contracts running at one time. People within an organization may belong to several different project groups at the same time. Some people may belong to one main team, but may be seconded to a committee which meets three or four times per year.

If you belong to several different teams it is inevitable that some conflicts will arise. Typical areas where these might occur include:

» **time** – teams may need you at the same time;

» **location** – you may be needed at one location but be available at another;
» **confidentiality** – you may have access to confidential items of information which should not be shared with members of the other teams in which you are working;
» **loyalty** – you may find out some detrimental confidential information about someone who does not know it exists and you may not be able to tell them;
» **responsibility** – you may have responsibility for a project which conflicts with the work of another team in which you are working;
» **priorities** – you may have work to do for several teams with a restricted amount of time to do it;
» **hierarchy** – your team leader in one team may be your subordinate in another team;
» **competition** – you may be a member of two teams who are in competition with each other; and
» **competitors** – you might be in a team composed of your competitors. Organizations often supply their competitors with services and thus you could find yourself temporarily working with them. For example, British Airways carries out engineering on Virgin Atlantic aircraft.

In these circumstances it is necessary to:

» be quite clear which team you are working in at any one time;
» agree priorities with team leaders when workloads conflict; and
» recognize the boundaries of your role in each team.

EMPOWERING, ENABLING, OR WITHHOLDING POWER

Essentially, this debate is about how much authority to make decisions is going to be given to the team. We saw earlier in this chapter that giving authority and responsibility can be a very motivating factor for the team. However, when deciding how much authority we give the team, there are other important considerations.

We should begin with the customer. Here are some of the key questions we should ask ourselves.

» How long should customers be expected to wait for a response to an enquiry or problem?
» How long do they have to wait when dealing with our competitors?
» How complex is the problem and where in the organization are the skills and knowledge that can solve it?
» Where in the organization *should* the skills and knowledge be?
» Are there any implications for other customers?
» Are there any concerns for the organization as a whole in terms of resources or policy?
» What are the implications if the solution turns out to be incorrect?

The heading of this section offers three main options, so let's look at what they mean in some more detail.

» **Empowering** – ensuring that the team has the necessary competence to make decisions and passing down authority to them to make them.
» **Enabling** – ensuring that the team has the necessary competence to make decisions, but requiring them to seek authority before the final decision is made.
» **Withholding power** – requiring decisions to be referred upwards.

Peters and Waterman (1982) refer to "simultaneous loose tight properties," which means keeping some of the core values of the organization under tight central control, while allowing some degree of freedom at the customer interface in respect of other values which are not so critical.

Thus, an airline might allow its cabin crew to make customer service decisions on the spot according to their own judgment; on the other hand, any safety regulations would have to be carried out to the letter, with no authority being given to the crew to vary them.

Another way we can look at this issue is to consider two main factors:

» How complex is the decision in terms of implications for the other customers or for organizational resources and policies?
» How urgently does it need to be made?

This will give us four main combinations.

» **High complexity/high urgency** – the decision needs to be made quickly; it is, therefore, important that the skills and knowledge to make it are contained in the team which is dealing with it. The decision is also very complex, which may mean that there are implications for other customers or for the organization as a whole. *Enabling* the team will allow it to come up with a solution which can then be checked quickly by higher authority for its customer/organization implications.

» **High complexity/low urgency** – the decision does not need to be made quickly so it is not necessary for all of the skills and knowledge to be available within the team because there is time to seek further advice. As the decision is very complex, possibly with significant implications for future policy or long-term resource planning, *withholding power* might be a prudent course in this case, with the decisions being made at higher levels.

» **Low complexity/low urgency** – the decision does not need to be taken quickly so there is time to refer it upwards. However, as it is not very complex, with few implications, *enabling* or *empowering* could be the appropriate options.

» **Low complexity high urgency** – the decision requires a quick resolution and has few implications, so the team might be *empowered* to make the decision on their own authority.

This is demonstrated in Figure 6.2.

Herzberg (1966) recognized responsibility and achievement as being powerful motivational factors. Empowering teams by giving them more responsibility is likely to result in them becoming more motivated. If the team is successful and adds achievement, then this may give them an added fillip.

Full empowerment is often withheld from teams because people further up the hierarchy are reluctant to relinquish power; they see it as a loss of control over the organization.

Certainly, if a team is given the power to make decisions, it will use it, and it may not always use it in the way the organization expects it to. However, as long as people are fully trained and the limits of their empowerment are clearly defined, it can be a very powerful force.

It takes a lot of confidence and trust in the team, and in the skills and knowledge that the members have gained, to empower them to any

Increasing
complexity

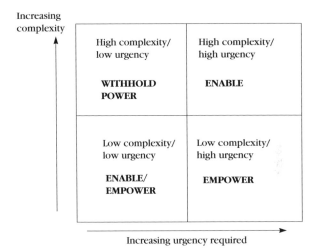

Increasing urgency required

Fig. 6.2 The complexity/urgency matrix. This diagram first appeared in the autumn edition of *Training and Competence News* and is the copyright of George Green. It is reproduced with permission.

great extent. There has been a general trend towards enabling instead, which allows speedy responses but also retains more control.

When making decisions, the team needs to have a system by which it decides which is the best course of action. It may simply be that the leader consults team members and then makes the decision. If the team members are going to make the decision together, then there are numerous methods, each with its advantages and drawbacks:

» **majority decision** – the decision has a lot of support and can be made quickly, but this doesn't mean it's the right one;

» **full consensus** – means that everyone supports the decision and owns it, but it may take a long time to ensure that every team member agrees;

» **go with the team member with most expertise in the area for the decision** – uses the most important resource, but others may not buy into the solution; or

» **sticking with what it says in the rule book** – no-one can be blamed, but is it what the customer wants?

The method chosen could be written into the team's charter if it has one.

It is also important that, as part of their development, team members have the opportunity to become familiar with a range of problem-solving and decision-making techniques, though these are outside the scope of this volume.

KEY LEARNING POINTS

» Teams can be a strong force in bringing about change but can be equally powerful at resisting it.
» Teams need to be motivated to perform well.
» There are a variety of methods of developing teams and team members.
» Teams sometimes get it wrong.
» Attention needs to be paid to being an effective team member.
» Consideration must be given as to the degree of responsibility given to teams.

Team Development Success Stories

This chapter includes case studies of:

- » North American Space Agency and Russian Space Agency;
- » The Republic of Ireland's soccer team; and
- » Raffles Hotel, Singapore.

In this chapter we look at three examples of organizations that show successful application of some of the concepts we have met in our analysis of developing teams. Each has a slightly different focus.

» The North American Space Agency (NASA) and the Russian Space Agency (RSA) have moved well beyond being global organizations, as they now have some of their teams in space. We look at the co-operation between Russian and American teams on the Shuttle-Mir space station project.
» The Republic of Ireland soccer team performed exceptionally well in the 2002 World Cup finals. We look at some of the concepts that lay behind their performance.
» The world-famous Raffles Hotel in Singapore is renowned for its service. We look at how its teams delight its customers.

Let's begin by looking at an example of teams who used to be fierce competitors but are now working in close co-operation.

CASE STUDY: NASA AND THE RUSSIAN SPACE AGENCY (RSA)

We have looked at team working from a number of aspects in this volume, including globalization. Now, we will look at team working across the void of space. One of the most enthralling rescues in the twentieth century involved NASA's mission control team, working mainly from Houston in Texas, USA, and the crew of Apollo 13, under the command of Jim Lovell, when they had a malfunction on their journey to the Moon. Once the initial disappointment had sunk in that they were not going to be able to land, it soon became apparent to everyone involved that it had become a matter of survival, some 200,000 miles out in space.

That they did survive was a result of several factors, including:

» the dedication and brilliance of the mission control team on the ground, who persevered to find solutions as each new crisis developed;
» the determination and skill of the crew;
» the attention to detail; and
» the bond between the crew and everyone involved in the program.

The details of the emergency are well documented, especially in the book *Man on the Moon* by Andrew Chaikin (1994).

Since the heady days of landing on the Moon, of course, the exploration of space has moved on.

The introduction of the Space Shuttle allowed resources to be reused, thus lowering costs, and opened the way for scientists to go routinely into space to carry out experiments. While the moon landings had involved only American crews, albeit with a wide range of suppliers from around the world, the latest ventures have involved collaboration with other countries to the extent that the International Space Station is being built through the efforts of a number of nations, including the US, Russia, many European nations, Japan, Canada, and Brazil. In this case study we will look at the Shuttle-Mir program, which was the first phase of the International Space Station and was developed by Russia and the US.

Essentially, the program was set up to learn more about what is involved in establishing a space station. There were four main goals:

» to learn how to work with international partners;
» to reduce the risks of developing and assembling a space station;
» to gain experience on long-duration missions; and
» to conduct life science, micro-gravity, and environmental research programs.

We can focus mainly on the first goal here, which concerns team working.

We will look at the following aspects in more detail:

» culture;
» language;
» decision making;
» team interaction.

Culture

Russia began its space exploration as a part of the Soviet Union. Since the Union broke up, in 1991, Russia has found it more difficult to finance the space program. It is also more complex now as its space port at Baikonur is in Kazakhstan, and some of its booster rockets are also made in the Ukraine, each now a nation separated from its previous "parent" in the Union.

Russia has a well-educated population and great ethnic diversity, stretching, as it does, from the borders of Eastern Europe and Scandinavia, right across to the Pacific Ocean.

We mentioned Trompenaars' dimensions of culture in Chapter 5; he notes some significant differences between the US and Russia. For example, the past tends to be more important to Russian people than to Americans, though for both the future is seen as most important. Also, in the US, people expect openness from their government, while Russia is only just emerging from a period when the government worked in relative secrecy.

Trompenaars' research also points out a number of similarities, however. For example, when asked if we should try to control nature, almost the same percentage of people in Russia (42%) as in the US (38%) felt that it was worth trying.

The cultural differences did lead to some misunderstandings during the Shuttle-Mir negotiations, but they were eventually resolved as the people came to know each other better.

Symbols can have great importance in culture, as we have seen. The people involved in space missions often design patches for their clothes that represent the mission. The design of the Shuttle-Mir patch represented the achievements of both nations working together and also their individual achievements.

Language

The Russian and English languages have a number of significant differences, so it is not that easy for Russians to learns English and for Americans to learn Russian.

In fact, both sets of crew did learn each other's language, but it is clear from what individual astronauts have said that they did not have any great depth of knowledge. Unlike the airline industry, which uses English as the working language, the Shuttle-Mir program actually kept both languages in use, so that all operational procedures were set out in both Russian and English. This was clearly in the interests of safety so that everyone on board had a clear understanding of what the procedures were.

Astronaut Shannon Lucid, for example, jokes on the NASA Website about the way in which she and her fellow cosmonauts spoke to each other. They used Russian, because one of them didn't speak English. "I know that a lot of the times I wasn't saying anything exactly correctly. But he was always able to understand what I was saying, so it was never a barrier." The cosmonauts, Yuri Onufriyenko and Yuri Usachev, joked back, suggesting that they were developing a new "cosmic language."

So, despite any language differences, the crews were clearly able to communicate with each other and even develop their working relationships further through the humor that arose from time to time.

Decision making

Early in the program, working groups were set up, consisting of experts from NASA, the Russian Space Agency and its partner Energia, the Institute for Biomedical Problems, the Gagarin Cosmonaut Training Center, and other organizations. They divided the mission tasks into nine different functions, one for each group. The US and Russia each had a co-chair for every group, who chaired joint meetings and signed protocols that documented agreements that had been made. Before each joint flight, all operations were written into joint agreements.

There was no overall center in charge of everything – the mission control center in Houston controlled the Shuttle, while the mission control center in Moscow controlled Mir. The commander of the Shuttle was responsible for the vehicle and its crew, while the Mir commander had responsibility for the space station and its crew.

Joint flight rules were developed before each mission, covering contingency responses for unusual situations, the implications of which had already been reviewed. The idea was to reduce the need for any split-second decisions that had not been fully thought through. In the event, the collision with the unmanned supply vehicle Progress did mean that some real-time decisions had to be made, as we shall see later.

Co-ordinating the two control centers was quite a challenge, as they were separated by distance, time zone, culture, and language. Systems and procedures were set up to facilitate this and a strong working relationship was built up through simulating real-life situations.

Team interaction

Here we can focus on one particular incident – the collision with Progress on June 25, 1997. Michael Foale gives an excellent account of what happened and how he felt about it on the NASA Website:

"After the collision, Mir went into a slow spin, which meant that its solar arrays could not pick up any energy from the sun, with the result that the batteries went flat, so many of their systems went down, while others were shut down to conserve what energy there was. Among the systems that were down were the oxygen-generating system and the carbon dioxide removal system.

"There was also a leak and they were losing pressure, but the crew managed to isolate it and stabilize the pressure. It was only after they plugged the leak with a hatch that they realized how significant an emergency it had been.

"And still was. . . "

It was about this time that some very important decisions had to be made by Foale and his fellow crew members, Vasily Tsibliev (the station commander) and Aleksandr Lazutkin.

Mission control on the ground needed to know quickly what the rate of spin of the station was. Foale found himself reacting rapidly; he and put his thumb against the window and looked at the stars. He estimated a spin of one degree per second and informed mission control. They accepted his word, backed up in a second call by Lazutkin, and made the necessary corrections from the ground to stop the spin. This was the first time that Foale had made an operational intervention on Mir.

A second problem occurred; they needed to spin the station back into position using their own Soyuz capsule, designed for returning the cosmonauts to Earth. The problem was that no-one on the station really knew how to do this and the contact with the ground was immediately lost, so they were on their own.

Foale had some ideas and because, in his own words, "I was puffed up that they'd accepted my measurement on the rotation rate," he put them forward, even though the responsibility for the station was the station commander's. Foale understood rotation dynamics because he was a physicist, so he made some suggestions. He admits that he wasn't totally sure it would work. He realized that his colleagues were beginning to listen to him and he was afraid that he might just not know enough to ensure that the correct action was taken. They spent some time discussing what to do.

They finally decided to try short bursts to see what effect that would have and then to work out from that what the next move should be. It was very complicated and it took them three hours, communicating with each other from various parts of the station. However, they managed to improve the orientation of the station and were able to get their systems back on line.

Here is an excellent example of a crew, in adversity, pulling together and working with each other to find a solution to a critical problem. It's another example of synergy at work, as no-one individually knew the absolute right answer for certain. Together, they figured one out.

It is also an example in which the crew used its own knowledge and skills to find a solution to a problem which was not in the procedures and there was no mission control available to give advice or instruction.

Value of the program and the lessons learned

Foale suggests that the greatest benefit from the Shuttle-Mir program was the increased understanding that was developed between the Russian and the US teams, which can be taken forward to the International Space Station. Although some very useful technical information was gathered, this was insignificant in comparison with the team-building issues.

The last US astronaut to leave the Mir station, Andy Thomas, perhaps summed up the value of the program best when he said, "The spirit of competition that has existed for forty years has evolved smoothly into a spirit of cooperation."

TIME LINE

» **1968–72**: Project Apollo reaches and explores the Moon.
» **1975**: Apollo-Soyuz test program marks the first co-operation between NASA and the Soviet Union, resulting in the first international human space flight.

» **1981**: Space Shuttle launched.
» **1986**: Space Shuttle program suspended after Challenger explodes, killing all seven crew members.
» **1988**: Shuttle program resumes.
» **1994**: Shuttle-Mir program begins with the US and Russia as partners.
» **1994**: Sergei Krikalev becomes the first Russian cosmonaut to fly on the US Space Shuttle.
» **1995**: First Shuttle docking with Mir.
» **1995**: Norman Thagard becomes the first US astronaut on Mir.
» **1996**: Shannon Lucid begins the continuous US presence on Mir.
» **1997**: Jerry Linenger becomes the first US astronaut to wear a Russian space suit on a space walk.
» **1997**: Mir is involved in a collision with the unmanned supply vehicle Progress.
» **1998**: Shuttle-Mir program comes to an end.
» **1998**: First construction flights of the International Space Station begin, requiring some 45 flights over a five-year period.
» **2002**: Shuttle flights postponed due to tiny cracks being found in some of the liquid hydrogen fuel lines leading from the orbiters into the Space Shuttle main engines.

Key insights from the case study

» There was a clear purpose for the program.
» Competitors can become partners.
» Culture is an important factor when setting up international teams.
» Symbols are an important ingredient in culture.
» Language can be a barrier to team communication, but it can be overcome.
» Sometimes, for the sake of safety, more than one language may need to be in use by an international team.
» Not all decisions that a team may have to make can be foreseen.
» Teams will pull together in the face of adversity or threat.

» The team interaction gains are seen by many people as more important than the technical gains of the program.

Now we can look at an example of outstanding team spirit.

CASE STUDY: THE REPUBLIC OF IRELAND SOCCER TEAM

The Republic of Ireland soccer team won its way through to the 2002 World Cup finals, which were held in Japan and South Korea. They came with a reputation for being very difficult opponents to overcome, though they were not among the favorites to win the competition.

Ireland had qualified for the finals from a very difficult group, which included strong teams such as Portugal and Holland. In fact, they had finished equal first in the group but had to settle for second place owing to Portugal's superior goal difference, with the result that they had to go through a play-off with the runners-up from another group, Iran. The play-off was over two legs and Ireland won by two goals to one over the two games, to qualify for the finals.

They were again drawn in a difficult group for the first round of the finals, along with Germany, Saudi Arabia, and Cameroon. Only the top two teams would go through.

However, before the tournament even began, there was a dispute between the coach of the team, Mick McCarthy, and its captain, Roy Keane. The conflict resulted in the captain returning home days before the opening match, and taking no part in the competition.

This was a severe setback for the team. Not only was Keane the captain, but he was also considered by many to be Ireland's most skilful player. Indeed, he is widely held by his peers and the media to be a world-class performer. The club with which he plays, Manchester United, had gone to some lengths to renew his contract with them, such was the regard in which he is held.

With the first game only a few days ahead, the coach selected a new captain and reorganized the team. Behind the scenes there were some negotiations to see whether Keane could, after all, be convinced to play, but they came to nothing.

It would have been understandable if the team had capitulated rather quickly after this turmoil and many people wondered how motivated they might be. In fact, the team rallied round the coach and each other and went on to perform well beyond the original expectations.

In each of their games they had a mountain to climb.

» Match One: Ireland vs Cameroon. Before Ireland played their first game, Germany had won by eight goals to nil against Saudi Arabia, thereby stating their intention to dominate the group. In Ireland's first game, against Cameroon, they trailed by a goal in the first half, but roared out in the second half and equalized. Many thought they deserved to go on and win, but a draw was a good result against highly skilled opponents.

» Match Two: Ireland vs Germany. Ireland went a goal behind to Germany, yet they played so well that it was generally thought that they deserved to win the match rather than lose it. Then, in the very last minute, they equalized to gain a draw. Considering that Germany went on to be finalists, this was an excellent performance. Many teams would have given up during those final moments, but not the Ireland team.

» Match Three: Ireland vs Saudi Arabia. Ireland now had the opportunity to qualify if they won their last match against Saudi Arabia by two goals. The challenge here was that Ireland had never scored two goals in the finals of the World Cup in their history. This time, they went on to win by three goals to nil and duly qualified to play Spain in the next round.

» Match Four: Ireland vs Spain. Spain were among the favorites to win the competition, so this match was a severe test – the team that lost would go out of the competition. Ireland trailed by a single goal scored early in the game. They came back strongly and played some very attractive football, but Spain defended well. Then Ireland had a chance to equalize from a penalty kick. When the penalty was missed most people thought that was the end. But, with almost the final kick of normal time in the game, Ireland were awarded another penalty. This time they scored, taking the match into extra time, with the score at one goal each. There was no further score so the match eventually had to be decided by penalty kicks.

It was noticeable that, as the five players chosen to take the penalties were preparing, the coach, the rest of the players, the substitutes, and those who had been substituted all held hands in a long line of mutual support. Sadly for the Irish team, the dream ended there as the Spanish team scored more penalties and went through to the next round.

Mc Carthy was full of praise for his players, who had not only put in some tremendous individual performances, but had also shown courage and determination as a team and displayed great team spirit. They had played for each other, supported each other, and had never given in.

If we look at some of the concepts, we can see several of them at work in this case study.

Team evolution

Losing their captain, who was also one of their most skilful players, was an early setback for the Ireland team. It looks as though the team was certainly in the "storming" stage during that period and actually had to re-form. Some individual players might have also gone into the "mourning" stage at this point. There was probably a further short "storming" stage as negotiations went on about whether the captain would be restored, but then, with its new captain, the team moved swiftly through "norming" into the "performing" stage. After the final match, the team members will "adjourn", though several of them are likely to be included in the team for future competitions.

Team motivation

There were several motivating factors at work for the Ireland team:

» they knew clearly what their objective was and the coach and the team really believed that victory was attainable;
» high levels of praise were given to the team by the coach and the media;
» challenging their competitors directly – you can't be much more direct than a penalty shoot-out;
» expectancy theory – they wanted to progress in the competition and thought that if they really put in the effort they could do so (their final defeat was all the more bitter as a result); and

» the team responded well to adversity, rallying round each other and their coach.

Leadership

The coach and new captain certainly focused on each of Adair's three circles:

» task – the tactics were clearly thought out and everyone knew what had to be achieved;
» individual – each team member was supported by the captain and each other, especially the five penalty takers at the end;
» team – the team spirit that was generated allowed it to be a highly effective team.

Pool/squad approach

All of the teams at the finals had a squad of players from whom the teams for each game could be selected. Each person trained and practiced with the team and was part of the whole team. This allowed teams to cover for injuries, loss of players' form, and changes in tactics.

Synergy

The team performed even better than it could have been expected to with the individual talents and skills that it contained.

TIME LINE

» **October 6, 2001**: Ireland qualify for the play-offs by finishing second in their group to Portugal on goal difference.
» **November 15, 2001**: Ireland defeat Iran in the play-off to go through to the World Cup finals.
» **May 23, 2002**: Ireland captain Keane goes home from the team's World Cup training headquarters after arguments with team coach McCarthy.
» **June 1, 2002**: Ireland draw with Cameroon in their first game.
» **June 5, 2002**: Ireland draw with Germany after a last-gasp equalizer.

» **June 11, 2002**: Ireland defeat Saudi Arabia to go through to the next round.
» **June 16, 2002**: Ireland draw with Spain after extra time and go out of the competition after a penalty shoot-out.

Key insights from the case study

» The importance of team spirit.
» The various stages of team evolution through which the team passed.
» Leadership focused on the task, the individuals and the team.
» There were a variety of motivational factors.
» The advantages of using the pool/squad approach.
» Synergy can result in the team performing even better than might be expected.

Finally, in this chapter, we can look at how an excellent organization creates the climate in which its teams can consistently perform to the highest standards.

CASE STUDY: RAFFLES HOTEL

Raffles Hotel in Singapore is one of the most prestigious hotels in the world. Both its luxury and its history mark it out as somewhere special for people to stay. It is now part of Raffles International, which comprises a number of deluxe hotels around the world. Competition for Raffles does not so much come from other hotels in Singapore, but from other outstanding hotels world-wide.

Raffles' mission statement was changed after its refurbishment of the late 1990s to reflect two strands:

"Raffles is Singapore's great historic hotel,
delighting patrons with many memorable experiences."

The hotel and its management want people both to enjoy themselves and to feel the history that the hotel exudes. Its reputation for excellence extends world-wide and its customers come from all parts of the globe. Over the years it has been host to some very famous people including actors and writers such as Somerset Maugham, Charlie Chaplin, Jean Harlow, and Ava Gardner.

There are a number of concepts at work.

» **Myths** - there is a legend that the last tiger in Singapore was shot under the table in Raffles' Billiard Room in 1902. The fact that the room was, at the time, on stilts, and that the tiger (which had escaped from a circus) was shot *under* the actual room, rather than within it, makes no difference to the people who visit.

» **Symbols** - the whole hotel is symbolic of a glorious past, from the decor and the names of the public rooms (such as the Tiffin Bar), to the uniforms of the staff. These shared symbols help the staff to identify with the purpose and the values of the hotel.

» **Legends** - the hotel was particularly famous during World War Two as British families congregated there from all over the Malaya Peninsula, before the fall of Singapore. In 1990, the hotel published a collection of stories entitled *Fables from the Raffles Hotel Arcade.*

» **Rituals** - the Long Bar is famous for its peanuts. The ritual is that the customers eat peanuts with their drinks (perhaps a famous Singapore Sling) and then throw the shell on the floor, which is soon covered in a thick layer of debris.

Seamless service

There are some 15 restaurants and bars at the hotel and the teams of chefs and serving staff in each of them are, like all of Raffles' employees, highly trained in:

» the knowledge of what Raffles means to its customers;
» the skills to carry out their own particular role to perfection; and
» the attitude of going the extra mile for the customer.

For example, the guest arriving for afternoon tea receives seamless service from beginning to end, beginning with the welcome at the door, through to being escorted to their seat, and ordering their beverages.

There is usually a vast buffet of wonderful food prepared by top class chefs, to which guests help themselves, though some dishes will be served for them. Whenever they return from a visit to the buffet, they find their table spotless, any remnants of cold tea having been cleared away, and a clean cup ready, and a member of the serving team poised ready to offer them a fresh drink.

Each member of the team can feel confident in the ability of other team members to perform their jobs to perfection. This type of service can only be delivered by teams of people who really understand their customers, their jobs, and their own responsibilities within the team. Certainly it is the sign of a team which is in Tuckman's performing stage.

The whole performance is carried out so unobtrusively that guests don't even realize it is happening.

Training

All staff receive training about the history and background of the hotel, as well as in customer service. There are also management trainee programs to prepare people for leadership roles. Training and development are regarded as investments rather than costs.

In 1998, the hotel was awarded the prestigious National Training Award by the Singapore Productivity and Standards Board.

Motivation

There is a very low turnover of staff at the hotel and there is a lot of competition for any vacancies that arise. The prestige of working for such an excellent organization is certainly likely to satisfy any self-esteem needs that people have. Also, the knowledge that, day in and day out, they are achieving what is required of them goes a long way to motivating them.

The security of working for such a significant employer is also likely to play its part.

Quality circles

Raffles operates quality circles, called Service Focus Groups, which are cross-functional and include team members from different departments so that any problems can be seen from a variety of perspectives. They meet each week to analyze current issues and to identify possible future concerns. Senior managers act as a steering committee for these focus groups.

Guest appearances

Raffles regularly invites some of the top chefs and vintners of the world to present a themed occasion. This was inaugurated in 1995, with a gathering of some of the world's finest Michelin-starred chefs and award-winning vintners providing Raffles' Annual Wine and Food Experience.

This not only provides a delightful event for customers, it also gives the permanent staff the opportunity of working with some of the most skilled people in their profession and of being involved in something different and vibrant. Success tends to breed success and learning from people who do their job to perfection can be even more useful than learning from mistakes; it is certainly more interesting and enjoyable!

TIME LINE

» **1887**: Raffles hotel opens; it has 10 rooms.
» **1899**: The main building is completed and the hotel begins to attract the rich and famous.
» **1902**: The last tiger in Singapore is killed under the elevated Billiard Room.
» **1921**: Somerset Maugham makes his first visit.
» **1931**: The proprietors go into receivership.
» **1933**: Raffles Hotel Limited is formed.
» **1941**: The hotel is used as a meeting point for British families during World War Two.
» **1945**: The hotel becomes a temporary transit camp for released prisoners of war.
» **1986**: Raffles celebrates its centenary a year early, because it is the year of the tiger.
» **1987**: Raffles is designated a national monument by the Singapore government.
» **1989**: The hotel closes for refurbishment.
» **1991**: Raffles reopens, fully restored to its former glory.
» **1991 on**: Raffles receives a string of awards from the travel trade, hotel guides, travel writers, and travel associations.
» **1997**: The hotel celebrates its 110th anniversary.

> » **1998**: Raffles is awarded the National Training Award by the Singapore Productivity and Standards Board.

Key insights from the case study

- » The importance of a team having a purpose, and valuing it.
- » The part played by myths, symbols, rituals, and legends in the organization's culture.
- » Effective team work requires each team member to be clear about their own role.
- » When a team works at a very high level of performance, customers will be delighted with the results.
- » Training and development underpin a successful team.
- » Motivation is crucial to persistently high levels of performance.
- » Quality circles allow problems to be viewed from a variety of perspectives.
- » Varying what the team does will bring interest and excitement into the task.
- » It can be very valuable to introduce top-class performers from time to time so that the team can learn from their success.

Key Concepts and Thinkers

The development of teams has a very wide range of concepts. This chapter includes a glossary of the terms that are used, including:

» explanations of the most common terms; and
» key writers and thinkers.

There are many concepts used in team development, proposed by numerous theorists. In this chapter, we look first at some of the terms that are used when analyzing teams and then go on to look at some of the key concepts and thinkers on the subject. Details of the works produced by these theorists can be found in Chapter 9.

GLOSSARY

Activity learning – A learning process that focuses on people carrying out activities and learning from them. This can be very useful in developing teams because it allows interaction between team members, from which a lot can be learned through the process of plan, do, review.

Coaching – Working with someone to improve their competence, often carried out on a one-to-one basis. In sport the term "coach" is often used to refer to the person who guides the team in tactics and selects the team from a squad for each game.

Competence – Having the necessary knowledge, skills and attitudes to carry out one's job effectively.

Culture – The ways in which a team behaves, including its symbols, trappings, myths, and celebrations.

Functional role – The role that a person takes in a team because they have the appropriate knowledge, skills, and attitudes that the role requires.

Development – Preparing people for future roles.

Development gap – Those additional skills, knowledge, and attitudes that people need to carry out their future role.

Development plan – A plan to ensure that people attain the appropriate levels of competence for future roles.

Extranet – A private Internet-like network service that is available between trading partners.

Group-think – The result of teams becoming too confident in their decision-making abilities.

Human relations school – A group of theorists, commencing with Elton Mayo, who recognized the importance of human elements such as socialization and motivation in increasing productivity.

Internet – The World Wide Web, which provides huge amounts of information, services and advice.

Intranet – A private Internet-like network service provided solely within an organization and unavailable to outsiders.

Leader – Someone who has the responsibility for ensuring that the team works effectively together and meets its objectives.

Matrix organization – An organization in which teams are set up with a range of knowledge and skills that enable them to take most of their decisions within the team and without the need to refer upwards, thus providing a faster response to their customers.

Member – Someone who works as part of a team. The term indicates a sense of "belonging."

Methods of training – The variety of means available to train and develop teams.

Mission statement – A broad statement of the organization's purpose and/or values.

Motivation – Creating a climate in which people want to give their best for the team.

Natural team role – The role that a person is likely to play in maintaining the cohesion and determination of a team. They were first identified by Meredith Belbin, whose team roles are discussed in more detail later in this chapter.

Quality circle – A team drawn from several different functions within an organization, whose remit is to consider issues of quality and to find solutions to problems concerning quality.

Risky shift – The possibility of a team making more risky decisions because there is no single person who can be held responsible.

SMART objectives – Specific objectives that are established from the mission statement. They allow teams to be quite clear about what they have to achieve; they also enable teams to know when they have achieved a particular objective. There are several variations of SMART, including:

» specific;
» measurable;
» agreed/achievable;
» relevant/realistic;
» time bound.

Squad system – A pool of team members who are available to provide their services when required; not all members are needed on a particular project at any one time. It is particularly prominent in sport, though also found in many other organizations.

Synergy – The team's performance is greater than the sum of each of the individuals working separately.

Team building – The process of creating a team and maintaining it at peak performance.

Team charter – A set of guidelines agreed by the team about how they will interact together.

Team evolution – The stages through which a team is likely to pass on its way to peak performance. Tuckman's model of team evolution is discussed in more detail later in this chapter.

Team spirit – The power that is demonstrated when each individual team member is giving everything they can for the good of the team. It is closely related to synergy in that the end result is that the team achieves more than was thought possible, given the individual skills and knowledge of each team member. It has more to do with attitudes than with skills and knowledge.

Tracking systems – Systems that allow team members to keep in touch with each other or with the rest of the organization, when they are away from the team. They can be used to give advance notice of key issues that team members need to be aware of or for managing human resources and allocating particular work tasks or projects.

Training – Enabling people to acquire the knowledge, skills, and attitudes to carry out their current job.

Training gap – Those additional skills, knowledge, and attitudes that people need to carry out their current role.

Training needs analysis – The process of establishing what the current level of competence is within a team or an organization as a whole; this is compared with the competence that the team needs and any gaps are identified.

Video conferencing – A system which allows people to attend meetings while remaining in their own location. This is discussed in more detail in Chapter 4.

CONCEPTS OF TEAM DEVELOPMENT AND THEIR THEORISTS

We can group the key concepts of team development as:

» team growth;
» team leadership;
» team membership;
» team culture.

Team growth

This area was considered by **B.R. Tuckman** and embodied in his theory of team evolution (1965). As we saw in Chapter 2, Tuckman identified four stages through which teams are likely to progress:

» **The forming stage**. The team has just come together. Members watch to see what other people will reveal. They are very polite to each other and tentative about revealing very much about themselves.
» **The storming stage**. Some people will begin to assert themselves. They may feel that they have particular strengths and may feel they have observed weaknesses in others. They may share their views with others who they feel may be like-minded and small cliques may begin to form. These cliques may come into conflict with each other, while they may also leave some individuals feeling isolated. There may even be a challenge to the leader of the team at this stage. There is certainly a potential for conflict. A significant amount of energy may be spent on this in-fighting, as the team focuses on its own internal struggle, often losing sight of the needs of its customers.
» **The norming stage**. Once the storming stage has passed, the team begins to settle down. Roles are defined and the team becomes more organized. Rules, systems, and procedures are agreed. The team members begin to learn more about each other, including their likes and dislikes and their various strengths and weaknesses. They begin to support each other and to make progress towards their objectives.
» **The performing stage**. After a while, the team will become extremely effective. In this stage, everyone is working well together, playing to each other's strengths and making up for any weaknesses.

Trust builds up within the team. Tasks may be delegated to individuals or sub-groups.

The time that a team spends in each stage may be long or short depending upon the situation and the people in the team. The team may stick in one stage for a long time before moving on or it may revert to a previous stage.

People leaving or joining the team may bring it back to the forming stage and it may be necessary to spend some more time going through the storming process once more.

Good examples of reverting to forming/storming can be found throughout the world when political parties are defeated in elections. They often have to form new teams with the people who have managed to retain their seats and very often they will elect a new leader. They may spend a long time going through the storming stage in which there is as much focus on political in-fighting as there is on developing new policies to help them win the next election.

Most teams tend to go through these stages, so we should not be overly concerned if a new team soon finds itself deep in conflict as a natural result of entering the storming stage. However, a team that remained in storming for a significant period would be of concern, since it is likely to be focusing on itself rather than on its customers.

For teams in the forming and storming stage, team-building activities and a team charter might be very useful.

Team leadership

Paul Hersey and **Ken Blanchard** (1977) considered the maturity of each individual in terms of their **ability** to carry out a task and their **willingness** to carry it out. This produced four main styles:

» **Telling**. A directive style for low levels of ability and willingness.
» **Selling**. As maturity increases, the context and rationale will be explained to try to achieve buy-in.
» **Participating**. At high levels of maturity, team members' views are sought and taken into account.
» **Delegating**. At the highest levels of maturity, tasks are simply delegated.

Thus, a team leader will use different styles for different members of the team. For new entrants to the organization, for example, a telling approach might be used at first, while for experienced people a participating or delegating style might prove more appropriate.

John Adair, who has written extensively on leadership and team working, suggests in one of his theories that there are three intertwining circles which the leader needs to balance:

» task;
» individual;
» team.

There is clearly a need to complete the **task** and meet the agreed team objectives. However, if we focus too much on the task, we may lose sight of what is happening to individuals and the team as a whole.

It is very easy for team leaders to forget that the knowledge, skills and attitudes of **individuals** all need to be maintained and improved if the team is to grow in effectiveness.

The **team's** cohesiveness and evolution also needs to be considered. The task may be completed, but the team may have fallen back into the storming stage as a result. The team itself may have stopped developing.

So, the leader will focus on all three aspects, giving more attention to one particular aspect in certain situations. Thus, during periods when deadlines are not so tight, more time may be focused on individuals or on team building. When a deadline approaches it may mean all hands on deck to complete the task.

Team membership

As we saw in Chapter 2 and Chapter 3, **Meredith Belbin** suggests that, in addition to a person's functional role, they will also have a natural role that they will adopt when working in teams (1981). Each of the nine roles has a particular strength which will help the team to be effective, though it also has an allowable weakness, which is the reverse side of the strength. Thus, a shaper might drive hard to help the team to persevere in difficult circumstances, though he or she might also be quick to lose their temper and be blunt to the point of rudeness.

The nine team roles with their strengths and allowable weaknesses are given in Table 8.1.

Table 8.1

Role	Strength	Weakness
Co-ordinator	Ensures that everyone's view is taken into account.	May manipulate people.
Shaper	Drives the team to complete the task.	Prone to temper, blunt.
Team worker	Keeps the team in harmony, minimizing conflict.	May be indecisive.
Plant	Provides new ideas.	Some ideas may be very impractical.
Monitor evaluator	Ensures that all choices or options are considered.	May appear to be rather dour.
Implementer	Turns ideas into action.	May like things done in a particular way.
Completer finisher	Ensures that the task is completely finished off.	May not trust others to do it properly.
Resource investigator	Builds up contacts outside the team.	May become bored after initial enthusiasm.
Expert	Contributes deep knowledge on specific issues.	May only contribute in a specific area.

All of the roles must be represented if the team is to be highly effective, though some members will be able to perform more than one role. There will be some roles (their primary roles) to which they are very predisposed and some (their secondary roles) which they could perform if called upon.

There are also roles that a person should best avoid, because they will not perform it very well.

Belbin argues that people should not try to rid themselves of the weaknesses that come with their team role, because they may eradicate the strengths. Rather, the team should work together in a way that manages the weaknesses and plays to the strengths. Thus, a plant might not be called upon to introduce some very practical systems.

Belbin has produced a software program, Interplace, along with documentation and a video, all of which help people to identify their own individual team roles. It is possible, for a fee, to discover one's own natural team roles via the Belbin Associates Website (www.belbin.com). The program has many uses over and above this, for example, to analyze a team to see who is likely to perform each of the roles in the team. This will also allow the team to identify any roles which are not represented or are rather weak. This enables them to consider introducing someone who might be able to perform the role, at the next selection opportunity.

Team culture

As we saw in Chapter 3, four classic types of organizational culture were identified by **Roger Harrison** and developed by **Charles Handy**. They are:

» **Power culture**. Here most of the power rests with one person who tends to be involved in everything that goes on. They will take most of the decisions; most communications will be routed through them; people can often communicate directly with them and receive a response directly back, rather than using the traditional hierarchical channels.

Everyone in the organization tends to take actions and make decisions that they feel will be approved by the power figure. If the person is not available decisions will usually have to wait; but when they are available decisions may be taken with great speed, resulting in a very speedy service to customers. Individuals may try to impress the power figure in the hope of gaining some reward such as promotion.

» **Role culture**. This is very hierarchical and has rigid lines of communication, which run mainly up and down the organization. Thus, decisions tend to require escalation for authority and then be passed down again, taking a long time. Information from one part of the organization to another at the same hierarchical level will not pass horizontally, but rather will go up to the top of one line of authority, and then down the other line; any response comes back in the same manner in the reverse direction. Most people simply do their own job, which is clearly defined, and avoid treading on other people's toes as there are few rewards for standing out from the crowd.

» **Task culture**. Here people work in highly skilled teams. Lines of communication are very flexible and will usually be horizontal, with people giving and seeking information from the best available source. They are often empowered to make decisions within the team, with minimal direction from above, because they are highly competent. Leadership of the team may be entrusted to the person with the most expertise in a particular area or with a particular skill, rather than to the person of the highest grade.

» **Person culture**. This most commonly applies to a group of professional people who share common facilities and systems, but tend to work on their own. Professionals such as dentists, solicitors, or architects might have this type of culture. There is often a rather loose association, with decisions normally being taken by the individuals themselves unless they directly affect other people in the organization. Communication tends to be at a professional level concerning issues such as administration, professional procedures, and ethics.

Several different types of culture might be displayed in various parts of an organization.

The theorists **T.E. Deal** and **A.D. Kennedy** also worked in this area, suggesting that there were two factors which influenced organizational culture (1982):

» the degree of risk attached to the organization's activities; and
» the speed at which the organization receives feedback on how successful its strategies have been.

This produces four main types of organization.

» **High risk/quick feedback**. The tough guy, macho culture, which is usually found in organizations made up of entrepreneurs who are very energetic and are prepared to take risks. They may make a lot of money quickly for their organization, but may also incur huge losses. Life will be exhilarating but possibly stressful and burn-out is not unknown.

» **Low risk/quick feedback.** The work hard, play hard culture, found in companies producing a variety of fast-moving products which may also have people who are very energetic and get through a lot of work, making many deals and taking lots of decisions each day. However, the risks involved in each deal may be much lower. You win most, you lose some! Life is likely to be varied and exciting and will be attractive to high achievers.

» **High risk/slow feedback**. The bet-your-company-culture, mostly found in organizations that are involved in projects taking a long time to come to fruition. They will have invested an enormous amount of time, money, and effort before they know whether they have been successful. Drug companies, for example, may spend years testing a possible cure for a serious illness before they find out whether it is going to be effective. People attracted to these organizations are likely to have technical expertise in the appropriate field.

» **Low risk/slow feedback**. The process culture, found in highly regulated organizations, which tend to be rather bureaucratic. Industries such as financial services, health services, or transport might provide examples. They may focus on procedures and be relatively slow to change. They are likely to attract people who feel comfortable within an environment in which procedures and responsibilities are clearly defined.

Resources for Developing Teams

This chapter sets out the best resources for anyone interested in developing teams, including:

» books and articles;
» Websites;
» magazines; and
» institutes.

The following resources are referred to elsewhere in this book, or may prove useful in further researching the subject of developing teams.

BOOKS

Adair, J. (1979) *Action Centred Leadership*. Gower, Aldershot, UK.

Adair, J. (1986) *Effective Teambuilding*. Gower, Aldershot, UK.

Adair, J. (1990) *Great Leaders*. Talbot Adair Press, Brookwood, UK.

Armstrong, M.A. (2000) *Handbook of Personnel Practice*. Kogan Page, London.

Belbin, R.M. (1981) *Management Teams, Why they Succeed or Fail*. Heinemann, Oxford.

Belbin, R.M. (1993) *Team Roles at Work*. Butterworth Heinemann, Oxford.

Belbin, R.M. (1997) *Changing the Way We Work*. Butterworth Heinemann, Oxford.

Belbin, R.M. (2000) *Beyond the Team*. Butterworth Heinemann, Oxford.

Belbin, R.M. (2001) *Managing Without Power*. Butterworth Heinemann, Oxford.

Blake, R.R. & Mouton, J.S. (1985) *The Managerial Grid III*. Gulf Publishing Company, Houston.

Brinkerhoff, R. (1988) *Achieving Results from Training*, Jossey-Bass, San Francisco.

Chaikin, A. (1994) *Man on the Moon*. Penguin, London.

Deal, T. & Kennedy, A.D. (1982) *Corporate Cultures: The Rites and Rituals of Corporate Life*. Addison-Wesley, Reading, MA.

Gross, B.M. (1968) *Organizations and their Managing*. Free Press, New York.

Hamblin, A.C. (1974) *Evaluation and Control of Training*. McGraw-Hill, Maidenhead, UK.

Handy, C. (1976) *Understanding Organisations*. Penguin, London.

Handy, C. (1978) *The Gods of Management*. Souvenir Press, London.

Handy, C. (1989) *The Age of Unreason*. Business Books, London.

Hersey, P. & Blanchard, K. (1977) *Management of Organizational Behavior: Utilizing Human Resources*. Prentice-Hall International, New Jersey.

Herzberg, F. (1966) *Work and the Nature of Man*. Staples Press, New York.

Honey, P. & Mumford, A. (1986) *A Manual of Learning Styles*. P. Honey, Maidenhead, UK.

Huczynski, A. & Buchanan, D. (2000) *Organizational Behaviour*. Pearson, London.

Ishikawa, K. (1972) *Guide to Quality Control*. Asian Productivity Organization, Tokyo.

Kakabadse, A. (1982) *Culture of the Social Services*. Gower, Aldershot, UK.

Kakabadse, A., Ludlow, R., & Vinnicombe, S. (1988) *Working in Organisations*. Penguin, London.

Kirkpatrick, D.L. (1975) *Techniques for Evaluating Training Programs*. ASTD, Alexandria, CA.

Kirkpatrick, D.L. (1998) *Evaluating Training Programs: The Four Levels*. Berret-Koehler, San Francisco.

Kolb, D. (1979) *Organizational Psychology: An Experimental Approach to Organizational Behavior*. Prentice Hall, New Jersey.

Kotter, J., Schlesinger, L.A. & Sathe, V. (1986) *Organization: Text, Cases and Readings on the Management of Organizational Design and Change*. Irwin, Homewood, IL.

McClelland, D.C. (1961) *The Achieving Society*. The Free Press, New York.

McGregor, D. (1960) *The Human Side of Enterprise*. McGraw Hill, New York.

Peters, T. & Waterman, R.H. (1982) *In Search of Excellence: Lessons from America's Best-Run Companies*. Harper & Row, New York.

Peters, T. (1987) *Thriving on Chaos*. Pan Books, London.

Peters, T. (1994) *Pursuit of Wow! Every Person's Guide to Topsy-Turvy Times*. Macmillan, London.

Phillips, J. (1991) *Handbook of Training Evaluation and Measurement Methods*. Gulf Publishing Company, Houston.

Redding, J.C. (2000) *The Radical Team Handbook: Harnessing the Power of Team Learning for Breakthrough Results*. Jossey-Bass, San Francisco.

Torrington, D. & Hall, L. (1998) *Personnel Management*. Simon and Schuster, London.

Trompenaars, F. (1993) *Riding the Waves of Culture*. Economist Books, London.

Vroom, V.H. (1964) *Work and Motivation*, John Wiley, New York.

Whetton, D., Cameron, K., & Woods, M. (1994) *Developing Management Skills for Europe*. HarperCollins, London.

ARTICLES

Harrison, R. (1972) "How to describe your organization." *Harvard Business Review*, September/October.

Maslow, A. (1943) "A theory of human motivation." *Psychological Review*, **50** (No.4).

Mintzberg, H. (1975) "The manager's job: Folklore and fact." *Harvard Business Review*, **53**.

Tannenbaum, R. & Schmidt, W.H. (1973) "How to choose a leadership pattern." *Harvard Business Review*, May/June.

Tuckman, B.W. (1965) "Developmental sequences in small groups." *Psychological Bulletin*, **63**. (American Psychological Association)

USEFUL WEBSITES

Blackboard: Blackboard.com

Peter Honey: peterhoney.com

R.M. Belbin: belbin.com

WorkSmart: WorkSmart.com

National Training Awards: www.NationalTrainingAwards.com

Conference Call Services: www.conferencecallusa.com

WorldCueTraveler: www.worldcuetraveler.com or www.ijet.com

Companies and organizations whose Websites have been useful in researching this text include:

American Airlines: www.amrcorp.com

British Airways: www.britishairways.com

Chartered Insurance Institute: www.cii.co.uk

Coca Cola: www.coca-cola.com

Irish soccer site: www.irishsoccer.net.futuresite.register.com

McDonald's: www.mcdonalds.com

Médecins Sans Frontières: www.msf.com

NASA: www.nasa.gov
Raffles: www.rafflesHotel.com
Rolls-Royce: www.rolls-royce.com
Susan Ford Recruitment: www.sfrecruitment.co.uk
Totaljobs.com: www.totaljobs.com
Unilever: www.unilever.com

MAGAZINES AND JOURNALS

Creative Training Techniques Newsletter, Bill Communications, 50
  S. Ninth Street, Minneapolis, MN, USA.
Human Resources Development International, Routledge Journals
  Dept, 29 West 35th Street, New York, NY 10001-2299, USA.
Human Resource Development Quarterly, American Society for Train-
  ing and Development, 350 Sansome Street, San Francisco, CA, USA.
LearningCurve, International Data Corporation, 5 Speen Street, Fram-
  ingham, MA, USA.
International Journal of Training and Development, Blackwell Pub-
  lishers, 108 Cowley Road, Oxford, OX4 1FH, UK.
New Directions in Program Evaluation, School of Education, Greens-
  boro, NC, USA.
Performance Improvement, International Society for Performance
  Improvement, 1300 L Street NW, Suite 1250, Washington DC, USA.

INSTITUTES AND TRAINING BODIES

Institute of Development Studies: www.ids.ac.uk
Institute of Management: www.instituteofmanagement.com
Institute of Personnel and Development: www.cipd.co.uk
Institute of Work Psychology, University of Sheffield: www.shef.ac.uk
Irish Management Institute: www.imi.ie

Ten Steps to Making It Work

This summary chapter provides ten key steps to make the concepts work, which are:

» have a clear idea of the team's purpose;
» agree SMART objectives;
» organize the structure;
» select team members, taking account of the task that needs to be completed and the team dynamics;
» consider how and by whom it will be led;
» take account of team culture;
» motivate the team;
» give feedback on team performance;
» agree a training and development plan; and
» evaluate and repeat your successes.

In the previous chapters, we have examined a number of concepts that help us to understand how we can develop teams. Now we can look at ten key steps that need to be taken to ensure that teams both achieve full effectiveness and maintain it over a period. These can be used in any organization, whether commercial or not-for-profit, large or small, global or insular.

Most steps should be carried out in order, although Steps 3, 4, 5 and 6 could be carried out in a different order. You may, for example, wish to select the team leader before identifying team members.

In addition, it is possible that you might start with a team that is already formed, which you join as a team leader or team member. Certainly, if you work in a large organization with several departments and levels of hierarchy, you may find that teams can remain mostly intact for long periods, while new leaders or team members come and go at intervals. It may not, therefore, be possible to set up an altogether new structure as in Step 3, or to select exactly the team composition that you would like as in Step 4. Having said that, carrying out the remaining steps should enable the team to work as effectively as possible within these constraints.

STEP 1. HAVE A CLEAR IDEA OF THE TEAM'S PURPOSE

We found, in Chapter 2, that it is necessary for the team to have a purpose. If your organization has a mission statement, its purpose will be stated in it.

It can be useful for teams within the organization to agree their own mission statements which fit in with the overall one. It is also possible to set out the team's values, which reflect its culture, by incorporating statements such as:

» working in highly effective teams;
» giving value to customers;
» achieving the best return for shareholders;
» being environmentally friendly;
» keeping customers and employees safe; and
» offering employees the opportunity to develop their knowledge and skills.

All of these help to set out the broad parameters within which teams can operate.

STEP 2. AGREE SMART OBJECTIVES

Usually, successful organizations will define their purpose more clearly, so the next step is to identify some SMART objectives so that everyone knows what they have to achieve. These should be rolled out across the organization so that each team has a set of SMART objectives, the achievement of which will contribute to the organization's overall objectives.

For example, one of the overall objectives may be to achieve $20mn in sales; each of 10 sales teams might, therefore be given the objective of achieving $2mn of sales.

If objectives are agreed with the team rather than imposed upon them, the team members are much more likely to buy into them and to take ownership of them; in turn, they are more likely to achieve them. Objectives should be challenging, but realistic.

Agreeing objectives is more than just sitting with a team leader or team members and saying, "Well, you achieved $1.5mn sales last year so you can achieve an extra 10% this year, so that's an overall objective of $1.65mn; you can achieve that, can't you? Anyway, the Board has committed itself to an increase of 10%, so it has to be achieved." This will not necessarily bring the buy-in that you want.

It is more about working through with the team any changes that have been made and any new opportunities that have arisen so that it can be agreed where the extra revenue is coming from.

In committing itself to an extra 10% as mentioned above, the Board should have taken account of these changes and will probably have included them in their business plan.

This might include any of the following:

» because of some very successful advertising the customer base is significantly larger than last year;
» new technology has been introduced making it much quicker to process a sale, cutting down the time needed and allowing the salesperson more sales opportunities;
» the price of the product may have increased;

» the price may have been discounted leading to much higher sales;
» new products may have been brought to market; or
» a competitor might have ceased to offer the product.

The team is much more likely to buy in to the new objective if they have an idea about the changes upon which the new objectives are based. They may even feel that they can achieve *more* than the board's objective because they can see extra value in some of the new initiatives.

STEP 3. ORGANIZE THE STRUCTURE

It is important to know which teams are going to carry out which parts of the organization's business. We mentioned in Chapter 2 that there are a variety of organizational structures that can be used. Different structures will be appropriate for different strategic approaches.

If the organization's customers need quick responses, then authority for decision making needs to be passed down to as close to the customer interface as possible. This means setting up teams that have the knowledge, skills, and attitudes to make decisions without seeking higher authority each time.

If rules and procedures exist that, if incorrectly implemented, have significant implications, it may be necessary to have a more complex decision-making process with authority held much nearer the center of the organization, with relatively little room for maneuver at the customer interface.

Some organizations thrive on having teams that are working in competition with each other. A typical example would be a call center, where each team would vie to have the highest weekly sales total. Other organizations stress the need for teams to give each other mutual support, especially when the operations are spread over a wide geographical area, as in a multi-national organization.

You will also need to decide whether teams will be permanent, temporary, or flexible, as in Handy's "shamrock organization", which we met in Chapter 2.

STEP 4. SELECT TEAM MEMBERS, TAKING ACCOUNT OF THE TASK THAT NEEDS TO BE COMPLETED AND THE TEAM DYNAMICS

We have seen the importance of team dynamics and team roles in ensuring that the team completes its tasks and meets its objectives. It is important, when selecting team members, that all of these aspects are considered. If only functional roles are taken account of it is very possible that, while the team may be technically sound, it may not work well enough together as a team to make an effective contribution to the organization.

We mentioned above that you may find yourself leading a team that has been together for a while and you might not be able to make any changes to its membership. What, then, are the implications if there are gaps in either the functional or team roles, or if you find that the team dynamics are just not working? There are a number of options, depending upon whether the gap is likely to be short or long term.

For functional roles, there is the option of contracting people in who have those skills; this may be particularly effective when the need for the role will soon pass. For example, a particularly complex computer program might be needed at the beginning of a project, but not in the later stages, so an individual might be contracted purely for that stage. However, should the need continue right through the project, then it might be more effective to close the gap on a more permanent basis, either by recruiting a new team member who has the required knowledge and skills, or by developing a current team member.

As far as gaps in the natural roles are concerned, Belbin argues that the team will be at a disadvantage if the roles are not fulfilled. Thus, a team without a shaper might falter if it encounters difficulties. He also argues that people should not be asked to perform the role if it is not one of their primary or secondary roles. People would not normally be hired simply to perform a natural role, but it may be taken into account when recruiting a new member of the team; alternatively, someone might be seconded from another team in the organization for a while.

Of course, it is also possible to have too many natural roles in the team. For example, while the lack of a shaper might mean the team lacks resolution, too many shapers might mean that it spends a lot of the time in conflict.

If the team finds itself spending too long on self-oriented behaviours, rather than task- or team-oriented, then feedback and training for the team members concerned might be appropriate.

STEP 5. CONSIDER HOW AND BY WHOM IT WILL BE LED

We have seen a number of concepts relating to leadership. It is clear that effective leadership will play an important part.

Your choice of leader may be influenced by the following.

» What style of leadership you feel might be appropriate for a specific team, taking into account how competent they are and what type of environment they are working in. In several of the concepts that we have seen earlier, the ability to change one's style to take account of the situation and the needs of people in the team would seem to be important. So a flexible approach to leadership may be most effective rather than a fixed autocratic or democratic one.
» The attributes that people generally expect from a leader that we first saw in Chapter 2 – these include:
  » vision;
  » a sense of purpose;
  » listening skills;
  » integrity;
  » resolution;
  » clarity of thinking;
  » fairness;
  » availability;
  » flexibility to change their minds;
  » preparedness to get to know the team.
» The person's natural role. Does this particular team need someone who can drive them (shaper) or someone who can ensure they all show their talents (co-ordinator)? Or is it so vital to complete the whole task that only a completer-finisher will do?

Choosing a leader, then, needs careful consideration, though such care in selection is not always taken. Often the leadership is simply given to:

» the most senior person in the hierarchy – this will especially be the case in a role culture where everyone knows their place in the organization and seniority may be a significant factor in promotion to more responsible roles;

» the person who is considered to be the most competent at their current job;

» the protégé of the power holder in a power culture – the choice of leader may sometimes be a reflection of how well that person interacts with the power figure rather than an indication that the person is ready to take on a leadership role; or

» the person with the most familiarity or experience of a project.

As we have seen, however, there is a lot more to leadership than simply being good at one's job or having a good relationship with the manager. It does not automatically follow that the most senior or most competent person in their current job will be most effective as a leader. So, when selecting a leader it is important to include in the process some consideration of their potential to take on the role.

Once the leader has been appointed, it is important that they are given specific training in the knowledge, skills, and attitudes that they will need as a leader as well as any other functional responsibilities they may have.

STEP 6. TAKE ACCOUNT OF TEAM CULTURE

We mentioned the importance of team culture in Chapter 3 and elaborated upon it in Chapter 8. Clearly, the type of culture in your team will be affected by:

» the structure of the organization;
» the dynamism of its environment;
» how quickly it needs to respond to customers;
» to what extent it is governed by regulations and rigid procedures;
» the people within it, including the leader; and
» lines of communication.

If you need to respond very quickly to customer requests, then a role culture will be too slow; by the time the team finally responds, the customer will have gone elsewhere. Similarly, if you are working in an industry in which there is rapid change, role cultures may find their competitors developing new products before they have made a decision about what to do.

However, if your industry administers safety or financial systems, the role culture may provide the right amount of checks and balances so that any changes are introduced in an orderly way throughout the whole organization and are properly thought through.

Another aspect of culture also needs some thought. As a team develops, it will begin to have its own symbols, rituals, and ways of celebration. It is also likely that myths will grow up surrounding specific team members, which will be embellished over time.

Examples of symbols include:

» updating to the latest software as soon as it is available;
» driving a particular make of car;
» wearing casual or smart dress;
» having laptop or palm computers to stay in touch; and
» using a common language such as jargon.

Examples of rituals include:

» celebrating birthdays;
» celebrating end of projects or deadlines met;
» going out socially on a specific evening each week;
» finishing early on a Friday; and
» working at weekends.

Myths might surround one of the past leaders of the team, or they might relate to specific outstanding performances.

It is especially important to be aware of these symbols, rituals and myths if you are joining an already established team or taking on its leadership.

STEP 7. MOTIVATE THE TEAM

We saw in Chapter 3 and Chapter 6 that there are many different methods of motivating a team. The important factor here is to ensure that the appropriate method is used. This means getting to know the team so that you know what is important to them.

It may be necessary to motivate different team members in different ways too; what is important to one might not be so to another. One might thrive on being given extra responsibility, while others may prefer to be given more control over their work.

The importance of the work itself should also not be underestimated as a motivating factor; the more interesting and challenging it is, the more likely people are to be motivated by it.

Remember that, in these high-pressure times, it is easy to forget that work can be fun and enjoyment is allowed.

STEP 8. GIVE FEEDBACK ON TEAM PERFORMANCE

Most successful organizations have a performance management system, which includes regular feedback and appraisal interviews.

If we revisit John Adair's three circle model here, we can see that a team may fail to achieve its objectives because there is a problem with:

» the task itself – it may be too difficult or there may not be sufficient resources to complete it;
» an individual team member – perhaps an individual is not performing their own role satisfactorily; or
» the team as a whole – the team itself may not be working well together as it may have ceased to operate as a cohesive unit, or it may have fallen into group-think or risky shift.

If the task itself is the problem, then it may need to be redefined or additional resources may need to allocated. If the problem concerns individual team members or the team as a whole, then feedback should be given to those concerned.

Feedback should be given throughout the year and takes two main forms:

» motivational – giving praise for what has been done well; and
» developmental – identifying where performance could be improved.

It is important that both types of feedback are given, when the circumstances are appropriate. It is so easy to forget to give motivational feedback, especially if a team regularly performs well. Eventually, people will say, "Why bother? Nobody appreciates our efforts." Likewise, it is easy to shy away from giving feedback on unsatisfactory performance because we want to avoid conflict. This usually results in the performance deteriorating further.

Whichever type of feedback is being given, it should be specific and set in context so that the person knows exactly *what* they are doing well or what they are *not* doing well and, even more importantly, *why*. It should also focus on the behaviours rather than on the personalities of the people concerned.

Let's suppose, for example, that a team of researchers has produced a relatively shallow report for you, which does not provide the amount of evidence that you require. Telling the team that the report is "useless," or worse, that *they* are "useless," may make you feel better but it is not particularly helpful. It

» fails to say what is wrong with the report;
» fails to say if there is anything at all of merit in it;
» makes the team feel demotivated;
» may make the team angry; and
» fails to suggest what improvements could be made.

A more effective way may be to tell them that "the report was well structured and covered the relevant areas. However, to fulfill its purpose in helping me to make decisions, it needed a lot more facts and figures in the areas of . . . "

This is much more specific and allows the team to know exactly what they need to do to improve the report. It

» says what is satisfactory and why;
» identifies what is *not* satisfactory and why; and
» is not a personal attack on the team.

STEP 9. AGREE A TRAINING AND DEVELOPMENT PLAN

A training and development plan needs to be agreed with each team member. The plan should have SMART objectives so that the person can be very clear in what areas he or she wants to improve performance and by how much.

At least one of the training or development objectives should relate to the way in which the team member works in the team.

For example, there may be a team member who finds it hard to be assertive, with the result that his opinions (which are often well worth listening to) are usually ignored, often to the disadvantage of the team. Perhaps once in a month his view will win approval.

A plan could be agreed for improvement over a three-month period.

An objective could be agreed that the person wants to reach a situation where at least six of his opinions are acted upon by the team per month.

Methods of improving their skills in this area might include:

» attending an assertiveness course;
» being coached one-to-one by another person on the team who is quite assertive already; or
» role plays.

There may be several other methods.

Improvement can be monitored over the course of the plan and checked at the end of the three-month period to see whether the objective has been met. If so, a new training objective will be set; if not, a further improvement plan will be identified and put into action.

STEP 10. EVALUATE AND REPEAT YOUR SUCCESSES

It is very important that team objectives are reviewed regularly and not just checked at the end of the period. Regular reviews allow progress towards the objective to be established, so that any necessary changes can be made in good time if it becomes clear that the objective will not be met. The model we met in Chapter 6 should be particularly useful:

» plan;
» do;
» review;
» adjust.

However, some teams focus only on what has gone badly, so that they can make improvements for the future. Many people will tell you that we only learn from our mistakes. This can produce a rather negative mind set and lead to demotivation. Clearly we do need to learn from our mistakes but it is just as important to look at what has gone really well so that we can repeat our successes. It also allows other teams within the organization to learn from and be influenced by this success.

An organization that wants to succeed will create a climate in which teams share their successes with each other so that best practice eventually permeates through every level of the business. We saw a good example of this in the Raffles case study in Chapter 7.

KEY LEARNING POINTS

We have identified the ten key steps for developing teams. They are:

1 Have a clear idea of the team's purpose.
2 Agree SMART objectives.
3 Organize the structure.
4 Select team members, taking account of the task that needs to be completed and the team dynamics.
5 Consider how and by whom it will be led.
6 Take account of team culture.
7 Motivate the team.
8 Give feedback on team performance.
9 Agree a training and development plan.
10 Evaluate and repeat your successes.

Frequently Asked Questions (FAQs)

Q1: What is a team?

A: One definition of a team is "a group of people pulling together for a common purpose, which they value." You can find the rationale for this in Chapter 2.

Q2: Why are teams so important to organizations?

A: Because of the complexity and volume of processes and activities, a variety of knowledge and skills may be needed to deliver an organization's end product. This may mean that several people may be involved in a single process. Successful organizations recognize that the result will be better if these people support and co-operate with one another, through working in cohesive teams. You can find out more about this in Chapter 2.

Q3: Do teams always make better decisions than individuals?

A: Generally, they have more knowledge and skills at their disposal than an individual, so they may be better placed to make some decisions, but this will not always be the case. In fact, there are three specific situations we have seen, in Chapter 6, in which teams may make less effective decisions than individuals:

» risky shift – in which a team makes a more risky decision than each individual would have made themselves;

» group-think – in which the team believes in its own success so much that it feels that it can't ever be wrong, which can result in the team rushing headlong towards a disastrous course of action despite being given repeated warnings by others; and

» compromise – in which no one really achieves the solution they want.

Q4: How important is a leader to the team?

A: It is usually recognized as being a key role. You can find out more about leadership in Chapter 2, Chapter 3 and Chapter 8.

Q5: What is a natural team role as compared to a functional team role?

A: Natural team roles were identified by Meredith Belbin. They are the behavioral roles that a person would adopt in a team, while the functional role relates to the person's job specification. You can read more about natural team roles in Chapter 2, Chapter 3 and Chapter 8.

Q6: Our team spends a lot of time and energy travelling to meetings. What technology is available to us to try to cut this down?

A: You will find, in Chapter 4, a description of a number of tools available to teams as a result of e-technology, including network-based solutions and video conferencing.

Q7: We never know where our team members are because they travel around the world. Is there any way we can know where they all are at any given time?

A: One of the tools you will find described in Chapter 4 is a tracking system, which keeps track of the movements of all team members wherever they may be. You may also want to read Chapter 5 which covers the global implications of team working.

Q8: What methods are available to develop our team?

A: There are a number of options and theories on team development, which are detailed in Chapter 6.

Q9: What happens on a team-building event?

A: The answer really is almost anything that the organization wishes to include. Most team-building events are developed as a response to customer preferences or are directly tailored for a particular organization. You will find some typical examples in Chapter 6.

Q10: I seem to work on my own a lot, am I still part of a team?

A: Not all teams spend all of their time together. Many organizations have teams that are spread out throughout the world. There are a number of tools available to help them to keep in touch and to be effective members of their team.

Index

EXPRESSEXEC – BUSINESS THINKING AT YOUR FINGERTIPS

ExpressExec is a 12-module resource with 10 titles in each module. Combined they form a complete resource of current business practice. Each title enables the reader to quickly understand the key concepts and models driving management thinking today.

Customer Service Department
John Wiley & Sons Ltd
Southern Cross Trading Estate
1 Oldlands Way, Bognor Regis
West Sussex, PO22 9SA
Tel: +44(0)1243 843 294
Fax: +44(0)1243 843 303
Email: cs-books@wiley.co.uk

Printed and bound by CPI Group (UK) Ltd, Croydon, CR0 4YY

14/04/2025

14656902-0001